Nature's Hidden Patterns

Regular, Random, and Chaotic

By Rick McKeon

Copyright 2018 Rick McKeon

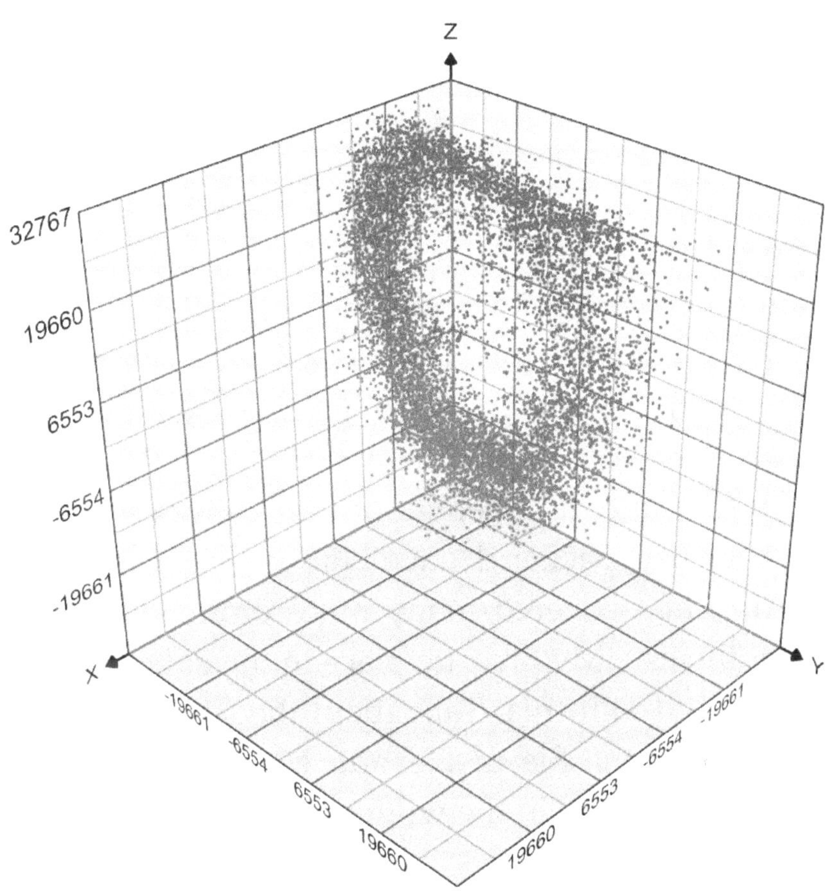

Preface

The natural world is filled with beauty and mystery. What we see on the surface is only part of the story. There are forces at work deep within. At first we get just a glimpse, but as we look deeper beneath the surface, we start to understand the heart of nature. Understanding these forces helps us to realize that we are meant to live in harmony with the natural world. Even more than that, we realize that we are part of nature and everything is interconnected!

When did this quest to find patterns start?

For me it was in the 1980's. What a wonderful time! Armed with degrees in mathematics and engineering, I was young and full of energy. The advent of the Personal Computer, Neural Networks, Chaos Theory, and affordable electronics parts for the hobbyist made that era so exciting!

I have always loved nature and being outdoors. I was a Boy Scout, a Scout leader, and an avid backpacker. I have climber Mt. Kilimanjaro, hiked in the European Alps, and covered many miles on beautiful hiking trails in the American Southwest. My favorite place in the entire world is the Sierra Nevada Mountains of California. Talk about the "flow state" and harmony! You will find them in the Sierra Nevada Mountains! The amazing and complex beauty that you find in the wilderness has always fascinated me.

Then one day an interesting thing happened.

My good friend and fellow math teacher Dan Zelasko and I were out hiking along the Cattaraugus Creek in Western New York. We took a little break and sat on a tree log that had fallen partially into the creek. It was during the spring melt, and the creek was raging! We could feel the log that we were sitting on move up and down in an unpredictable way and he said, "This is an example of chaos." I thought he might be right, but how can you know? The movement of the log seemed pretty unpredictable, but I had the feeling that deep down inside there were some coherent forces involved - some attractors.

If we can capture some aspect of nature's dynamic systems, maybe we can come to understand them better. In fact, just getting out in nature looking for these patterns will enhance your passion for this beautiful planet that we call home!

We'll talk about data visualization and graphical analysis later, but for now, just have a look at these interesting screen shots.

For the first one I wrote a BASIC routine to generate 10,000 random numbers, and then plotted them in two dimensions. No obvious pattern, right?

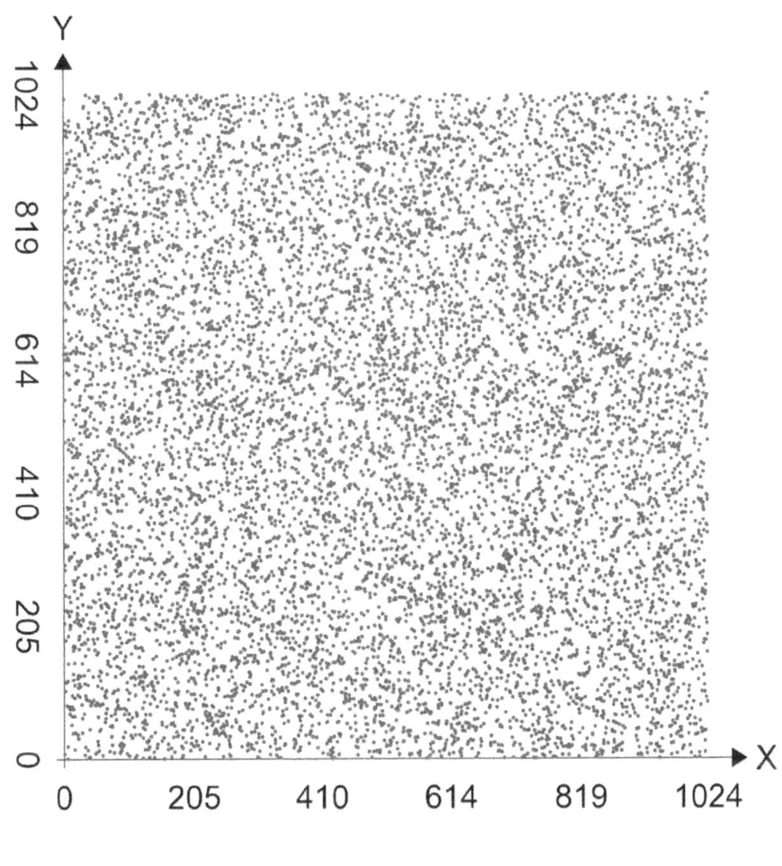

Random Pixels

The next picture shows data captured from a dripping water faucet. The scatter plot displays the captured string of numbers in three dimensions. While recording the drops I couldn't detect any obvious pattern, but when plotted in three dimensions a distinct pattern emerged!

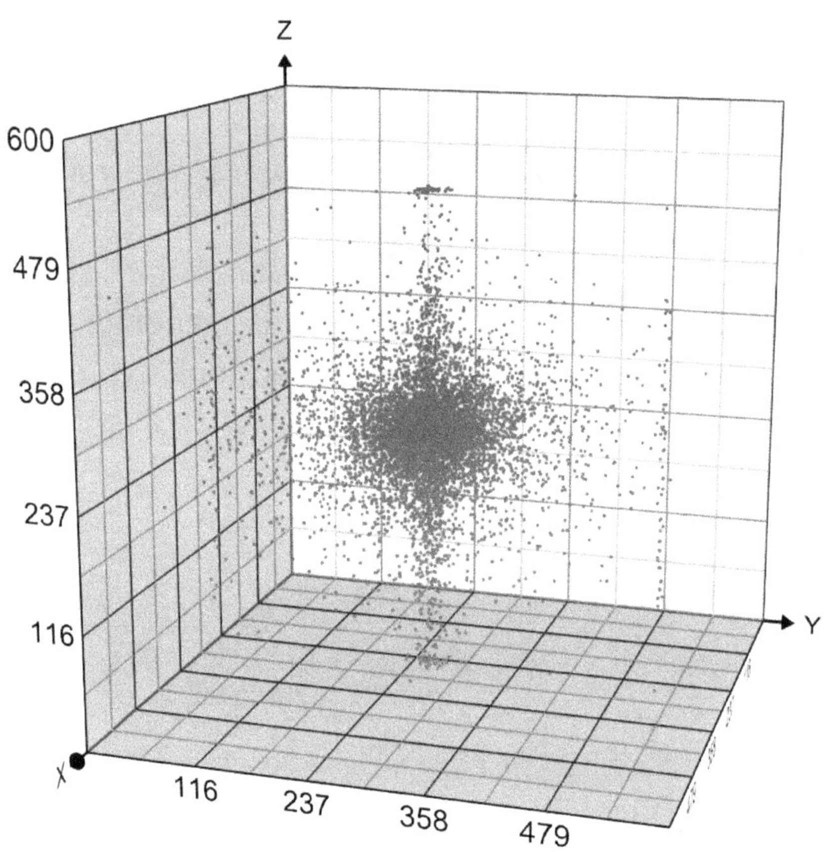

Dripping Water Faucet

Here's another interesting one. This plot was generated by capturing the sparkling gems of light being reflected off the surface of a lake.

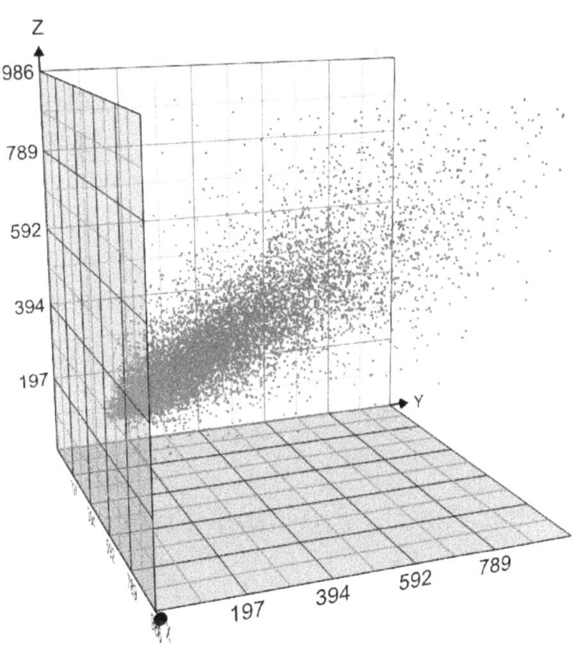

Reflections

We'll analyze these plots later, but I bet you already have some ideas about what is happening in each one.

We are going to have a lot of fun trying to understand things like wave motion, tree branches blowing in the wind, and the dancing flames in a fireplace.

The projects described in this book may not be highly precise and scientific, but they are lots of fun and easy to do. Hopefully they will inspire you to design some experiments of your own. We will design sensors to capture motion, sound, and light. Then we will write Arduino sketches to capture data and store it on an SD card, and then we will use some graphing software to display the data as 3-D scatter plots. We'll get out in the field and observe nature!

Even if you choose not to do the projects described in this book, I bet you will be inspired by the patterns we discover. For all of you "techie" types out there I have included code listings for the Arduino sketches together with the BASIC routines used for file conversion and random number generation. There are schematics and Fritzing diagrams for each experiment. Check the Appendices for all of the technical stuff. Also, all of the code listings are included on my website at rickmckeon.com for free download.

I don't have all the answers, but we'll have some fun speculating about where these patterns come from. I would love to hear your comments. Send me an email at rmckeon5@gmail.com.

Tips and Tricks

When you see this little guy, you know he is offering some interesting tips or just a silly comment to lighten things up.

Here's how each experiment will go. We will:

1. Capture some aspect of a natural event.
2. Clean up the raw data (if necessary) so it is useable.
3. Present this information graphically.
4. Look for patterns within the graphical presentation.
5. Try to understand the underlying forces involved.

There is a wonderful adventure waiting for us. So, let's get started!

Contents

Chapter 1: This Is the Age of Discovery

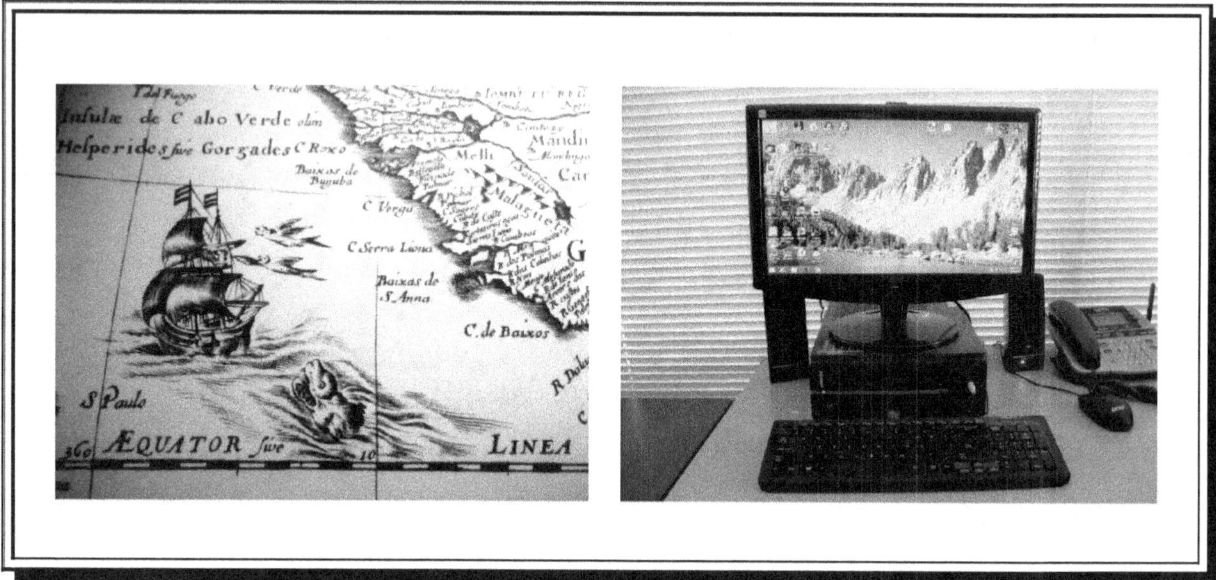

1.1 From Sailing Ships to PCs

During the early days of discovery explorers went out in sailing ships to find strange and exotic lands. The Royal Geographical Society in London would sponsor these hearty explorers and wait expectantly to receive their reports. Many of them were hailed as heroes or knighted by the Queen. What an exciting time!

Today is no less exciting. These are the days of exploration and discovery! The tools we use today are not the sextant and sailing ship. Our tools are small, inexpensive microcontrollers, sensors, and personal computers. You don't need to sail off to a far away land to make discoveries. You can make amazing discoveries in the woods near your home or even at the local city park.

Inventions like the telescope and the microscope expanded our understanding of the natural world. Today the average person can discover amazing things using commonly available tools like the Arduino microcontroller and the personal computer. These tools are very powerful and easy to use.

1.1.1 A Little History

In the early 1960's I was an electronics technician in the U.S. Air Force stationed at Ramstein Air Base in Germany. I used to fix the radio equipment used to support the planes on the flight line. Those were great times, but the electronics was pretty primitive. We're talking vacuum tubes.

I remember when the first "mini-tube" came out. They were so small compared to what we were used to. And then all electronic components started to be replaced with transistors and integrated circuits.

When I got out of the Air Force I went back to school and studied electrical engineering. We're still talking mid to late 1960s. Things were advancing rapidly with the development of the microprocessor, but product design was still pretty "low level."

In those days microprocessors required a lot of external hardware in the form of Random Access Memory (RAM), non-volatile memory to hold the program (EEPROM), Analog to Digital Converters (ADC), address decoders, and a bunch of other external circuits just to get the job done. Today we have Microcontroller Units (MCUs) with all that stuff on board. That simplifies things a lot! Also, we wrote our programs in machine language by hand (I mean pencil and eraser) on coding sheets using hex characters. A little later we got to write code in assembly language on a PC. That was a step up, but still pretty low level!

> Fast-forward 50 years.
> Wow, how things have changed!

Today we have powerful, easy to use microcontrollers like the Arduino and development systems that middle school kids become proficient at quickly. These technical advances have made it possible for the average layman or hobbyist to build interesting projects and discover amazing things!

We will use the Arduino and the PC (or MAC) to investigate the underlying forces at work in the natural world. We will study natural events and look for attractors. Dynamic systems may be attracted to a single point, a small set of points, or a beautiful complex shape called a "strange attractor." How exciting is that!

Our fieldwork will involve recording phenomena as diverse as a dripping faucet, wind blowing tree branches around, and reflections from the surface of a lake. You get the idea! Our curiosity about nature can be enhanced through the use of microcontrollers for data gathering and graphing software for display.

1.1.2 The Discovery Process

How does it happen? How do we go from an interesting question about the patterns in natural events to an insight?

Figure 1-1 illustrates the steps involved to go from a brilliant idea to an illuminating answer. Here's an overview:

1. We **ask a question** about some fascinating aspect of nature.

2. We **design an experiment** to collect data. The data capture may involve light, sound or movement. We may need to capture changing variables over time or simply try to capture the time intervals between events. At this point we also need to design the necessary jigs to hold the sensors. We may capture directly to the Arduino or to some other device like an audio recorder.

3. If we are capturing directly to the Arduino, we **write a sketch** to read the sensor data and store it to an attached SD card shield. This would typically involve taking readings every so many milliseconds.

4. If we are capturing to another device we will write the Arduino sketch after we have the data in a presentable form.

5. If necessary, we **clean the captured data** to make it useable for triggering interrupts.

6. With Windows File Explorer, we **create a folder** for the captured data on our PC. Then we read the data from the SD card and save it in that folder as a simple text file with one entry per row.

7. Next we use a BASIC routine to **convert that text file to a three-column comma separated (csv) file** that can be imported into our graphing software. Of course it doesn't need to be a BASIC routine. You could use any computer language you want for the file conversion.

8. Then the fun begins! We **plot that data set** out in three dimensions and look for patterns. Amazing patterns show up this way that would be impossible to spot just looking at a string of numbers.

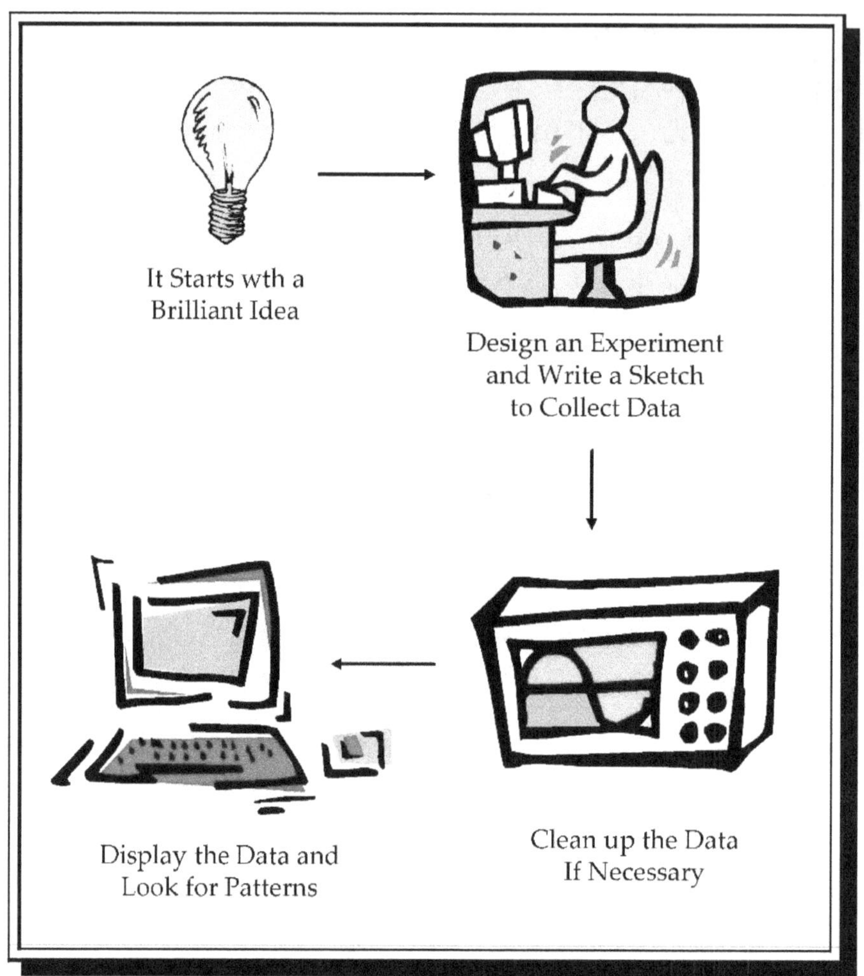

Figure 1-1. The Discovery Process

1.1.3 Two Different Approaches

If you think about the fascinating natural processes that we see all around us, you will notice that they seem to fall into two basic categories - Continuous and Discrete.

1. **Continuous:** Processes like the sound of a waterfall or the symphony you hear when hundreds of crickets sing together I call "continuous" because we can't detect individual sonic events within the process. All of the sounds seem to blend into one amazing chorus. Could there be any pattern, or is what we hear completely random? For these types of phenomena our approach will be to sample at regular

intervals and look for patterns in the overall experience. The graphical plots we discover contain many surprises! We'll spend some time trying to understand them.

2. **Discrete:** The second category I call "discrete" because it consists of a series of events that we can distinguish. They may be imbedded in a noisy environment but we can filter out the noise and capture the time intervals between the individual events. Examples of this type of event would include a dripping water faucet, claps of thunder during a storm, and raindrops on a tin roof from an approaching storm cell. First we need to isolate the events from the background noise and then we need a way to capture the time intervals involved. After that, we need a way to display these time intervals so we can look for patterns. Now we're talking about triggering interrupts on the Arduino to capture the milliseconds between individual events.

None of this is really hard, but you can see we have some interesting things to discover!

1.2 The Arduino

1.2.1 What Is an Arduino?

The Arduino is a microcontroller unit (MCU) mounted on a small circuit board. For these projects we will be using the Arduino UNO pictured in Figure 1-2 below. It has a built in USB port for connecting to the PC and connectors for easy access to the MCU pins. Not only do you have easy access to the pins, but also the pin names are printed on the board and on the headers, so they are easy to identify. The same headers allow for other boards called "shields" to be stacked on top of the basic Arduino. One shield in particular that will be important to us for data logging is the SD Card shield. An SD card can hold lots of data samples! We'll get into some detail regarding these pins as we work our way through the projects.

One of the important things about the Arduino is that it is easy to program. We will use a simple integrated development environment (IDE) on the computer to write the programs called "sketches" and download those sketches to the Arduino via the USB port.

The Arduino stores its programs in nonvolatile memory. Why is that so important? You can take it out in the field as a stand-alone data logger and collect all kinds of interesting stuff with it powered from a 9V battery. So, we're talking about simplicity and portability!

Another important thing is that the MCU used in the Arduino UNO is a very popular and well-supported chip from Atmel called the ATmega328. Now we're talking price, availability and support. Also, it will probably be around for quite some time. If you go looking for one, you won't get the message, "currently unavailable."

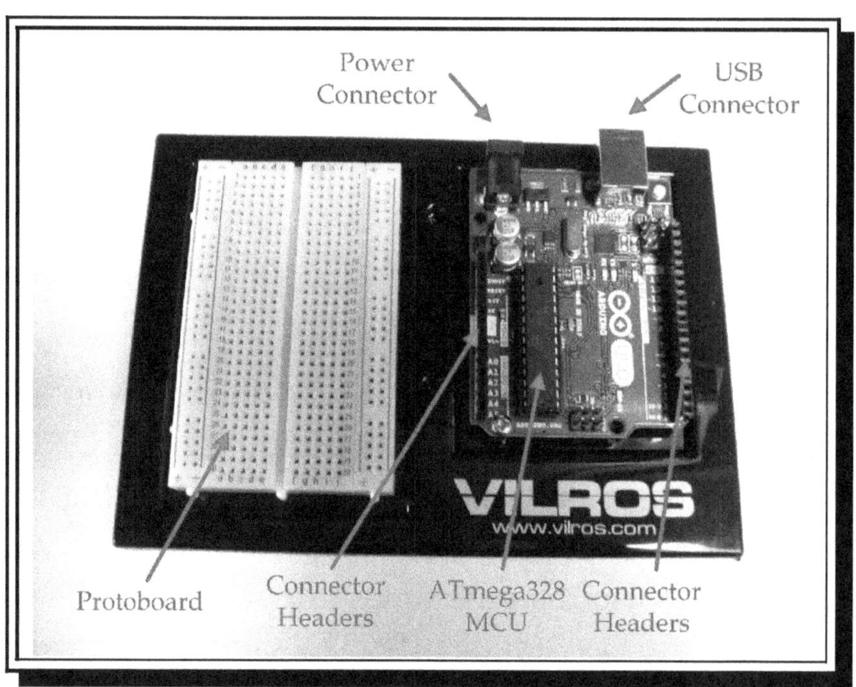

Figure 1-2. The Arduino UNO and Solderless Breadboard

We live in such an exciting age! Complex hardware such as the Arduino and so many other components are available to everyone at a reasonable price! Never has it been easier for the average hobbyists to build interesting projects and make original discoveries.

The Arduino has many and varied capabilities, but for the projects described in this book, we are going to use it mainly as a data logging devise. The sensors will supply information to either an analog or a digital port on the Arduino, and it will save the data to an SD card.

Once we have captured useable data, the sky is the limit!

Why use an Arduino?

1. It has counters and timers based on a very accurate clock that allow us to determine how long an event took or how many milliseconds have passed between events. How cool is that!
2. It has two interrupt pins (D2 and D3) that allow for Interrupt Service Routines (ISR) to be initiated immediately when triggered. This means that the trigger could happen at any time and the MCU will service it no matter what else is going on. We don't need to constantly check the input. It's kind of like the telephone ringing, "Are you going to answer that or not?" Well, the MCU answers on the first ring. So, if it needs to happen immediately we will use an interrupt. When the ISR is completed the MCU goes back to what it was doing. For our purposes that means just waiting around for the next interrupt.
3. There are simple commands to write data to an SD card that resides on an attached "shield." A shield is another little board that plugs

right onto the Arduino board. An SD card has lots of storage space and can be easily copied to a folder on your computer using Windows Explorer.

1.2.2 The Arduino IDE

The Arduino integrated development environment (IDE) is the software that we will use to write programs called "sketches" and upload them to the microcontroller. The IDE can be downloaded from:

www.arduino.cc/en/Main/Software

Arduino is an open-source project with an active user community. There are a huge number of tutorials available, and plenty of idea sharing. There are active Facebook groups, plenty of YouTube tutorials, and kits with projects to build available on amazon.com. In other words, it is well supported and lots of fun. The Arduino IDE is available for Windows, Macintosh and Linux operating systems.

Figure 1-3 shows a blank IDE screen. As shown in the figure, the sketch consists of two parts: the **Setup** and the **Loop**. Appendices A, B, and C show the Arduino sketches we will use to capture data.

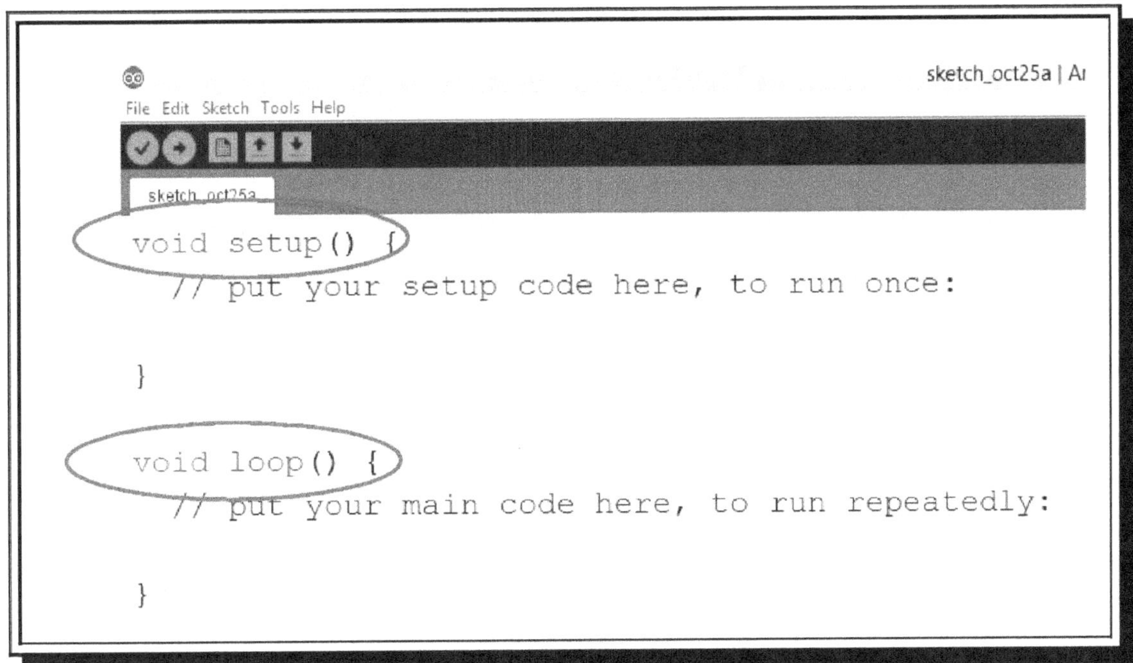

Figure 1-3. Blank IDE Screen

1.2.3 The Arduino as a Data Logger

You can use the Arduino to do many things. It can be used to monitor sensors and control robots, but for our projects we will be using it to capture data from natural events in real time. We will use it as a data logger in two different ways:

1. To capture and record data at regular intervals. This means taking a sample every so many milliseconds. We will be writing to a Class 10 SD card, so we can get around the loop and capture about 50 samples per second.
2. To capture the time intervals between events. This approach will be interrupt driven because we don't know when the next event will occur. That may sound complicated, but it's actually a very simple sketch.

You will become familiar with these two different approaches as we work our way through several fascinating projects.

For each project we will design an experiment and make a field trip to collect data. Hopefully you will be inspired to design some experiments of your own. Even if you are not handy with tools, I bet you will be able to build these simple jigs. Your imagination is the main thing. All the rest is finding a way to realize your vision.

1.2.4 The SD Card Shield

The Arduino has quite a bit of nonvolatile memory storage onboard, but an inexpensive SD card has a HUGE amount of storage capability (We're talking Gigabytes). Plus the information can be easily transferred to your computer using Windows File Manager and stored there as a text file. Once the file is stored on your machine, you can display it graphically and look for patterns. I'm always excited to see what kind of plot we will get. I may speculate ahead of time, but am often surprised at the interesting patterns that emerge! Each new plot will be a discovery! I'm going to ask you to guess what you think the plot might look like based on the captured event, but I bet many of them will surprise you!

Figure 1-4 below shows an SD card shield stacked on an Arduino UNO. It is called SD 3.0. I like this one because it can take a full sized SD card as well as the micro SD card. If you have a digital camera you are probably already familiar with SD cards. In fact, for these projects, I used the SD card from one of my cameras.

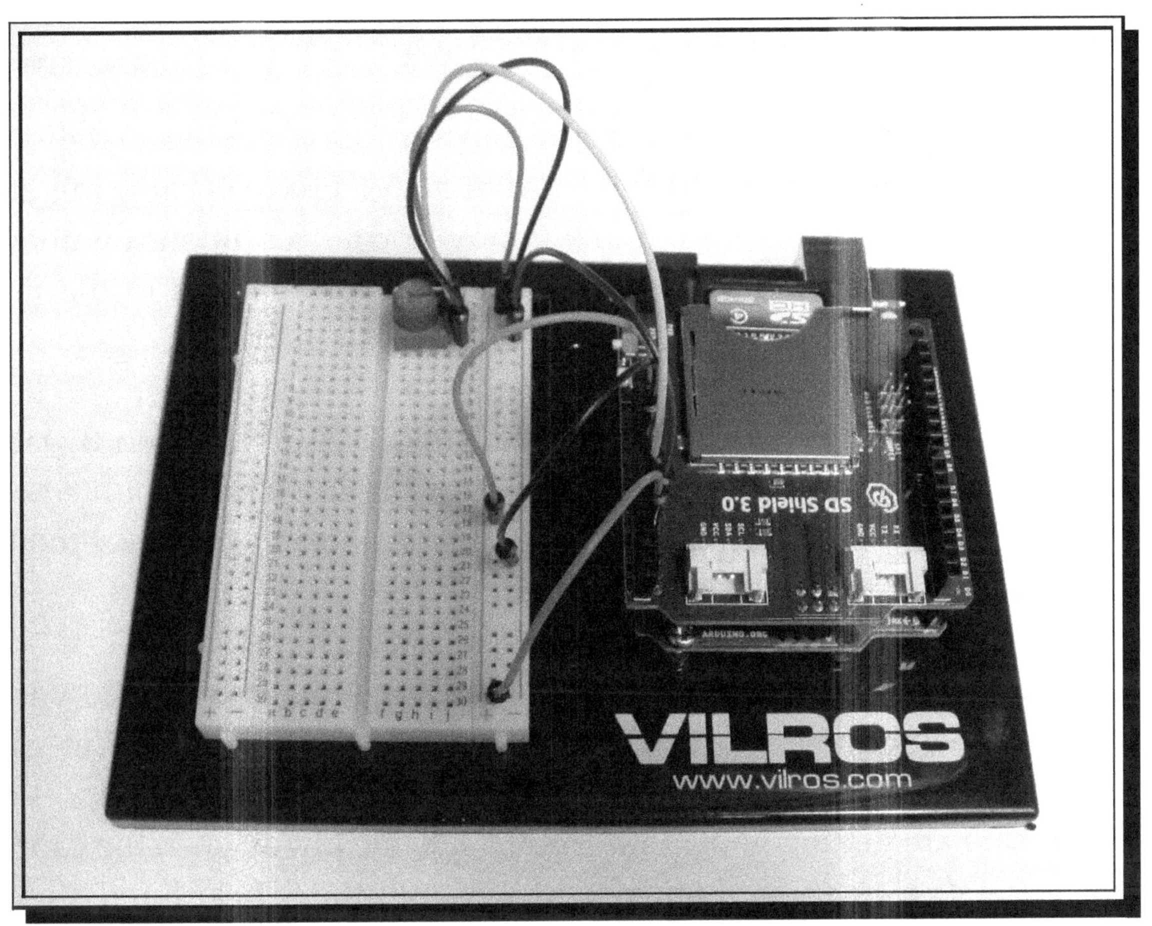

Figure 1-4. The SD Card Shield

1.2.5 My Arduino Workstation

Out in the field we want to capture information easily and accurately. We need the setup to be simple and stable. After all, you have to carry this stuff out to the location and set it up under windy or cold conditions on uneven ground. Maybe I sound like a wimp, but that's how it goes in the field. Give yourself every advantage - keep it simple and reliable.

So I built a little platform to hold the Arduino and a NuVision 8" tablet running Windows 10. It consists of a clipboard cut down and mounted on a tripod. I put some Velcro on the back of the Arduino and the tablet to hold them secure. It's simple, but it's stable and reliable.

The Windows tablet isn't actually necessary, but it makes the fieldwork a lot easier and puts my mind at ease knowing that I am capturing good data. I use it to start the capture and, by watching the Serial Monitor, I can tell that that I am getting good data. Also, it lets me know when the capture is finished. Once a capture is finished I will pull the SD card and stick in another one for the next capture. Figure 1-5 shows the setup.

Figure 1-5. My Arduino Workstation

1.3 The PC (or Mac) as "The Magic Lantern"

When I was young I had the pleasure of visiting "Expo 67" in Montreal, Canada. What an exciting World's Fair! One of the most intriguing pavilions for me was a presentation called "Laterna Magika" or "The Magic Lantern." It was a presentation that incorporated both film and live performers on the same stage. What a novel multimedia approach! Today I think the PC is the magic lantern.

1.3.1 QB64

We will use a simple BASIC routine to convert our one-dimensional capture files to three-dimensional csv files for plotting. This BASIC routine is shown in Appendix D.

QB64 will run on Windows, Mac OSX, and Linux. You can download it at www.qb64.net

We'll get into the details of working with QB64 as we work our way through the projects.

1.3.2 Graphing Calculator 3D

There are several free, open-source, graphing programs that you can use to create beautiful 3-D plots including GNU Octave and FreeMAT.

You can download GNU Octave at https://www.gnu.org/software/octave
You can download FreeMAT at www.freemat.sourceforge.net

For the plots in this book I used Graphing Calculator 3D because it is quick, easy to use, and creates beautiful high-resolution (4000x4000) plots. It is completely GUI (Graphical User Interface) based and doesn't require any coding experience. There is a free demo version available, but to produce any meaningful plots you will need to purchase a subscription to the Professional Edition. For more information about Graphing Calculator 3D visit https://www.runiter.com/graphing-calculator

1.4 Understanding Nature

Nature reveals herself in many fascinating ways. They involve sound, light and movement. There are many ways to explore nature and gain a deeper understanding of her secrets. One way is to capture information by converting nature's sounds and movements into numbers. Then we can analyze these numbers to gain an understanding from several perspectives.

1.4.1 Understanding What We Have Captured

I love all of the activities involved in these projects. I love to get out into the wilderness, look for interesting things, and try to capture some aspect of them. But the most interesting thing is to bring the data home and try to make sense of it. That's what the projects in this book are all about!

In Chapter 2 we'll set the stage with a discussion about regular, random, and chaotic events. Then in Chapter 3 we will roll up our sleeves and start collecting some data. So, hang on, the train is about to leave the station!

Chapter 2: Regular, Random, and Chaotic

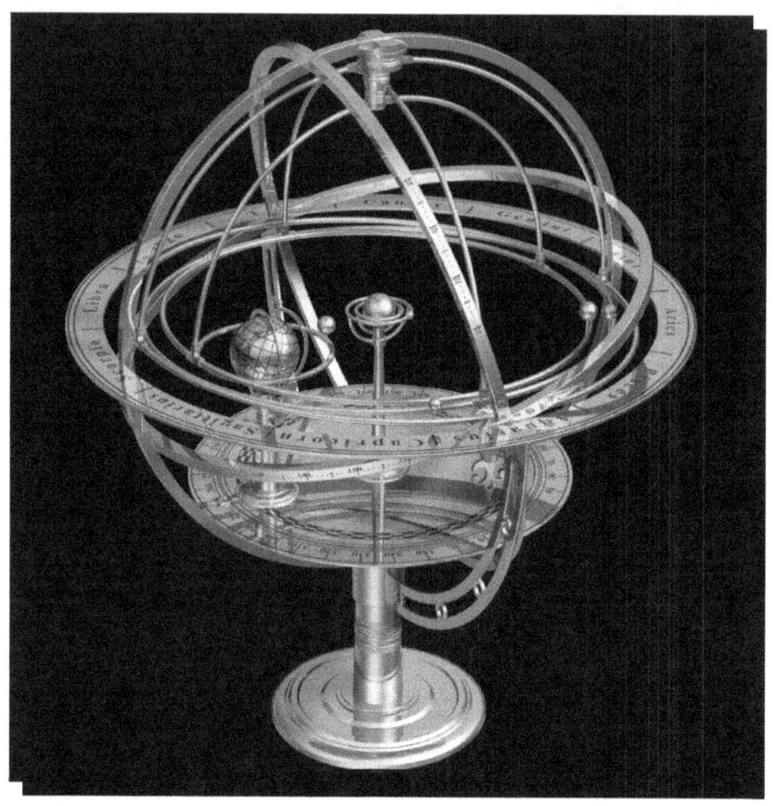

2.1 The Clockwork Universe

In the early days of science it was a popular belief that the universe obeyed certain mechanical laws and operated like a clock - very mechanical and very predictable. Sir Isaac Newton's laws of motion tended to support this view. It's a nice comfortable model. Who doesn't like things that are simple and predictable?

During my college days studying math and physics back in the 1960's we liked things that were "well behaved" and we dismissed things that had abrupt changes or behavior that we couldn't easily explain. These things were considered "anomalies" or "exceptions" that could be disregarded. That made things nice and comfortable. Life was good.

But, if you want to be honest, nature is not well behaved. It has too many complex and hard to explain things. It has too many abrupt changes and systems that run along smoothly for a while, and all of a sudden, become turbulent. You can't just disregard all of this stuff and think you are studying nature. Dynamical systems are unpredictable, but that doesn't mean they are random. They might be unpredictable in the short term and have underlying patterns that become obvious in the long term. There may be "attractors" involved. These forces push and pull things toward predetermined outcomes. Does that seem strange? Well, it is.

Here's an example. Think about a tree branch that is being blown back and forth in the wind. It may be moving in a crazy fashion as the wind gusts blow and change direction unpredictably, but there are also stabilizing forces at work. What happens when the wind slows down or stops? Just think about it for a while and you will realize that the structure and strength of the tree wants to return to its stable "home" position. It's kind of like the key signature of a song. It is continually drawn back to that "home place." A song may be in a major or minor key, but there is a note that the song is drawn back to. It's the place of rest or key of the song. Most compositions end on the "1 chord" to give the listener a sense of completion and finality. It's the same way for a tree. Its branches may be blown around, but there is a strong pull back to its place of rest.

Maybe we don't have the tools to understand everything in detail, but today we have wonderful tools to understand a lot more than we ever did in the past!

Many natural events appear to be completely random but there are forces at work that make them not random. They are instead, chaotic. Often we use the terms "random" and "chaotic" interchangeably, but they are not the same.

2.2 Simple and Complex Events

In the natural world you will find events that appear fairly simple, repetitive, and predictable. But you will also find events so complex that they seem to defy description. A swinging pendulum and the orbit of the moon around the earth are both very regular and predictable. On the other hand, rain drops or claps of thunder during a rainstorm seem completely unpredictable.

We are going to capture information from very complex events and look to see if there are any underlying patterns. If there are, we'll try to understand the attractors involved. I'm hoping that some of the experiments we do here will inspire you to go out and explore nature at a deeper level!

2.3 An Interesting Way to View Natural Events

One way to understand natural events is to capture some aspect of them as a bunch of numbers. These numbers might represent light intensity, sound volume, or motion. By just looking at a string of numbers you may be able to make some interesting observations, but to really spot patterns we need to somehow represent them graphically. The human brain is great at pattern recognition when it sees things presented in this way.

We are going to represent each of our captured data sets as 3-D plots in X/Y/Z space. This is one way to make patterns and relationships between the numbers stand out. So, how can we do this? I'll give you a quick overview here. As we do the various experiments it will all come together.

Let's have a quick look at how we can plot a one-dimensional string of numbers in three dimensions.

The data set we are going to capture is just a string of numbers. We call that one-dimensional list of numbers a **linear array**. How can you display a simple list of numbers in three dimensions? It turns out that it's pretty easy, and you don't need to be a math major to understand it!

As you probably remember from high school algebra, we can represent a number in space as a dot with the coordinate (x,y,z). This is illustrated in Figures 2-1 and 2-2. Sometimes it's difficult to see exactly where these points are because we are representing three-dimensional space on a flat sheet of paper, so I have shown them in two different views.

The four points in the graphs have coordinates (1,1,1), (2,2,2), (3,3,3), and (4,4,4). The point (1,1,1) is probably the easiest one to find. To find the point (1,1,1) do the following:

1. Come out the X-axis one square.
2. Then go in the Y direction one square and,
3. Then go up the Z-axis one square.

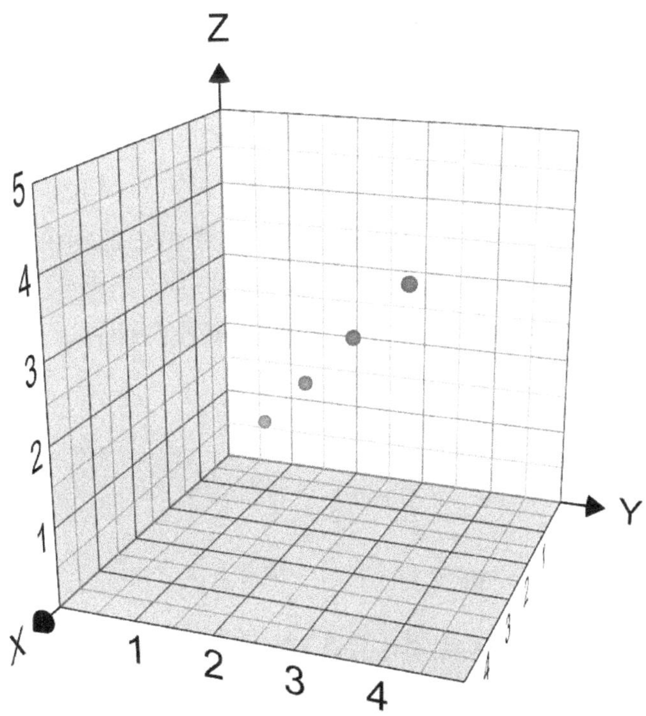

Figure 2-1. Points in X/Y/Z Space

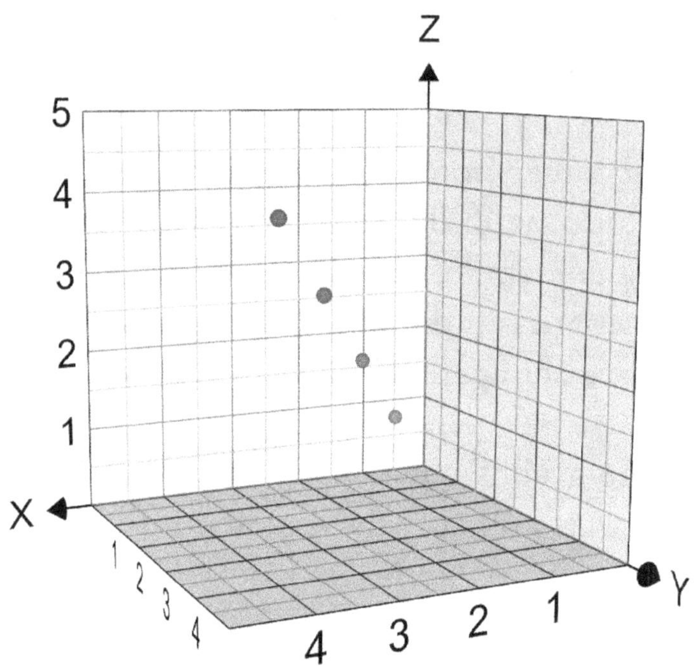

Figure 2-2. Points in X/Y/Z Space

OK, that's how we can represent a point using three numbers, but how can we take a string of numbers and represent then as (x,y,z) coordinates? Here's the trick.

Let's call our string of numbers n1, n2, n3, n4, . . . Here's how we are going to assign coordinates to all the points that we are going to plot:

1. Our first (x,y,z) point will be the first three numbers in the list (n1,n2,n3).
2. The next point will be (n2,n3,n4).
3. Then (n3,n4,n5). . .
4. See how it works?

It's like magic! We are representing a one-dimensional linear array in three dimensions. A simple yet powerful technique!

Now, we could make up our (x,y,z) coordinates as (n1,n2,n3) (n4,n5,n6) (n7,n8,n9) etc. and we would get a plot that looks similar, but using the first method gives a "stronger" plot because we get almost three times as many points from the same data set.

Of course, for many thousands of points this process would be pretty tedious. Our captured data sets will usually contain about 10,000 values, but - no problem - we'll let the computer do the work. We will use the simple BASIC routine shown in Appendix D.

2.4 Regular, Random and Chaotic: An Overview

The term "regular" is pretty intuitive. Events that are regular happen at predictable intervals. Examples would include the sun rising each morning or the ticking of a clock. If you are listening to a really good band with a groove you can tap your foot to the beat. You can get up and dance and it feels good. Waves washing up on the shore are pretty regular. A signal can be pretty complex and yet still be very regular.

Random and Chaotic are a little tougher to sort out.

Most people consider the terms "random" and "chaotic" to be the same, but they are very different. So, how can you tell if a system is random or chaotic? This discussion could get really technical really fast, but we're going to keep it fairly simple (I hope).

We can't just base our decision on predictability. In the short term both random and chaotic systems are unpredictable, but in the long term a chaotic system will display some kind of patterns.

You can toss a coin ten thousand times and not see any pattern whatsoever. In those ten thousand tosses you might get a string of heads coming up ten times in a row, and yet this is still a random system. The next toss might be another heads, or it might be tails. Even with a very large sample set you won't be able to discern any pattern except that the number of heads and tails start to even out or become the same. How strange is that! It's an example of a principle called, "The law of large numbers." But, flipping a coin is still an example of a random system.

So, here's the key.
Chaotic systems are "deterministic."

What the heck does "deterministic" mean?

Chaotic systems may be unpredictable, and they look very complex, but if you start at exactly the same place, and follow the same rule, you will get the same results every time. If you start in a slightly different place (I mean only slightly different) you will start out in a similar way, but it won't take long before it will diverge significantly. This is what's called, "sensitive dependence on initial conditions" or "the butterfly effect." It says that a butterfly flapping its wings in Japan can affect a hurricane in the Gulf of Mexico. Hard to swallow, I know, but there is such a thing as sensitive dependence on initial conditions. We see it in mathematics all the time. Also, you have probably heard the squeal that happens when an amplifier feeds back to a microphone. The initial noise is imperceptible, but it doesn't take long to grow out of control.

Frankly, I don't believe in The Butterfly Effect, but it is a good story to illustrate the nature of sensitive dependence on initial conditions. Sometimes positive feedback can be a problem!

With a random system you can start at exactly the same point and follow the exact same rules, but you will get completely different results every time.

That's why we are going to be looking for patterns. Natural events can be very complex, but usually there are some forces affecting how the system behaves. The forces that tend to affect dynamic systems in certain ways are called "attractors." It's as if they are attracting the components of the system like a magnet attacks metal or gravity attracts matter. In fact, gravity will be one of the attractors involved in most of the natural systems we are going to study. We'll capture information from natural events and see if any patterns emerge. How exciting is that!

In this chapter I'll introduce some waveforms created using a signal generator. Of course these are not "natural" waveforms, but we'll use them as part of the discussion about the difference between regular, random, and chaotic events. Figure 2-3 shows the inexpensive signal generator I used to create some simple, regular waveforms.

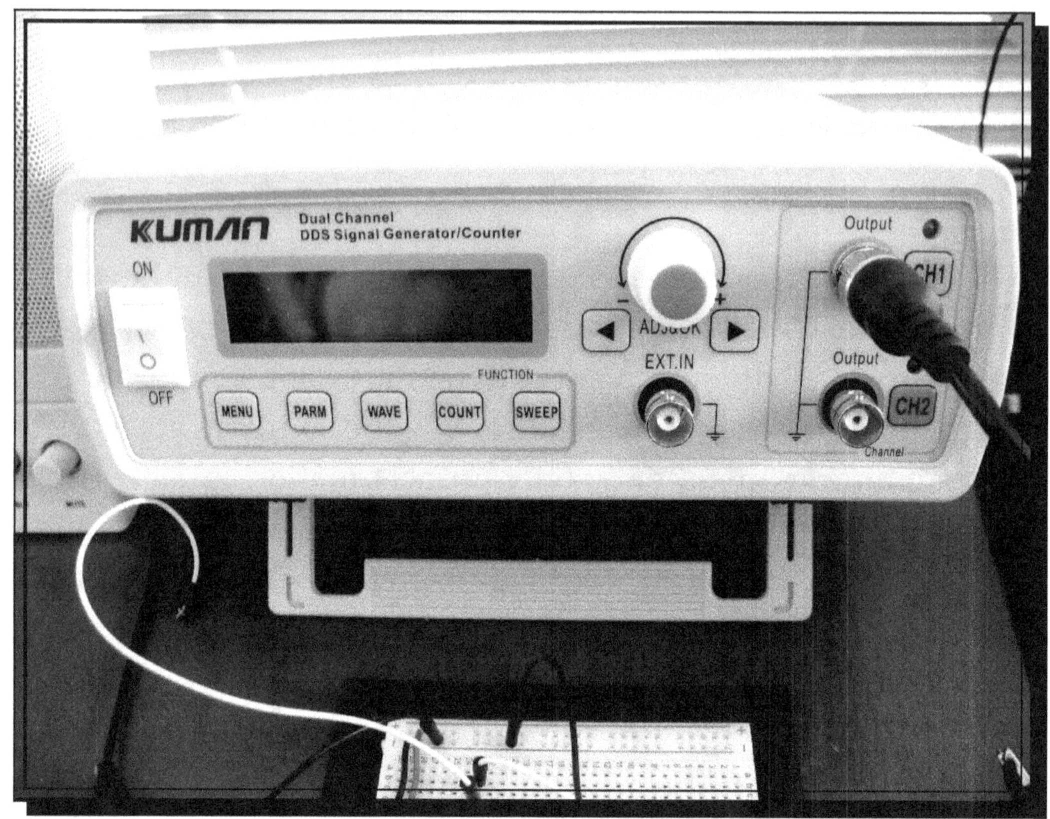

Figure 2-3. Signal Generator

This section is just a quick overview. We'll talk in depth about the different signals that we have captured as we work our way through the experiments. For now, just enjoy the different plots and see if you can figure out why they look the way they do.

2.4.1 Square Wave

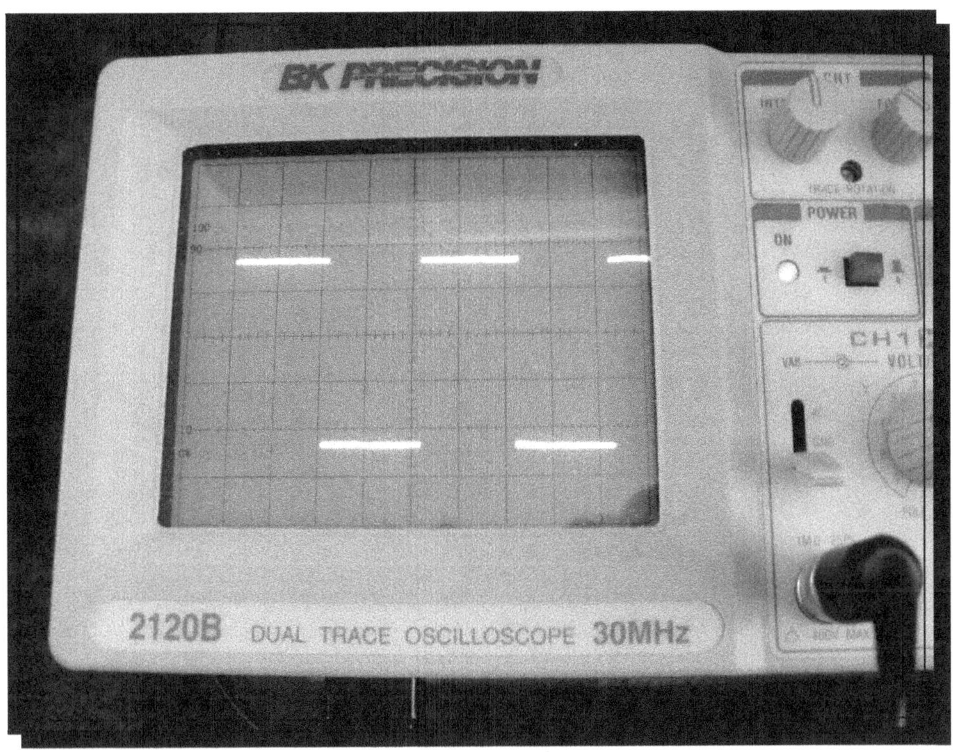

The square wave has to be one of the simplest functions. It is either HIGH or LOW. So it's binary. Now, think about it for a second - if we were to plot our sampled values for a square wave in three dimensions what would it look like?

The captured samples only have two different values. Let's call them HIGH (1) and LOW (0). So our (x,y,z) plot would consist of only eight points (0,0,0) (0,0,1) (0,1,0) (0,1,1) (1,0,0) (1,0,1) (1,1,0) and (1,1,1).

That's what we see in Figures 2-4 and 2-5.

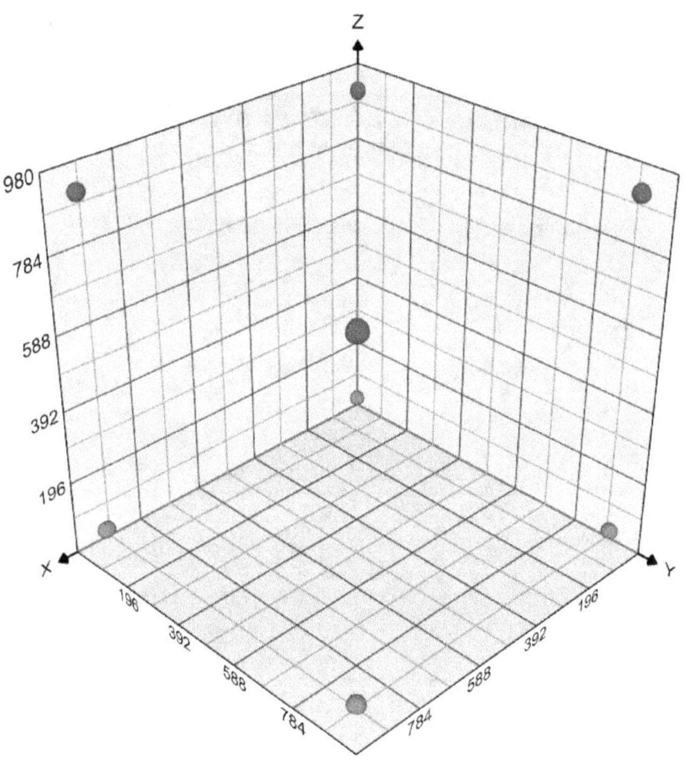

Figure 2-4. Square Wave, View #1

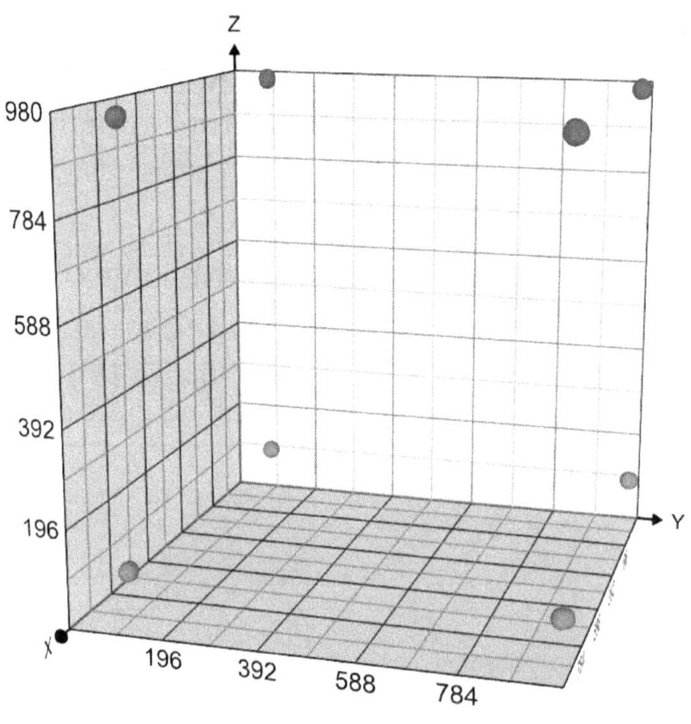

Figure 2-5. Square Wave, View #2

I was capturing a 4V p-p square wave with a 2.5V offset to put the voltages in a good capture range for the Arduino.

The Arduino captures voltages between 0V and 5V on its analog inputs as numbers between 0 and 1023. The sketch for capturing via an analog port is shown in Appendix A.

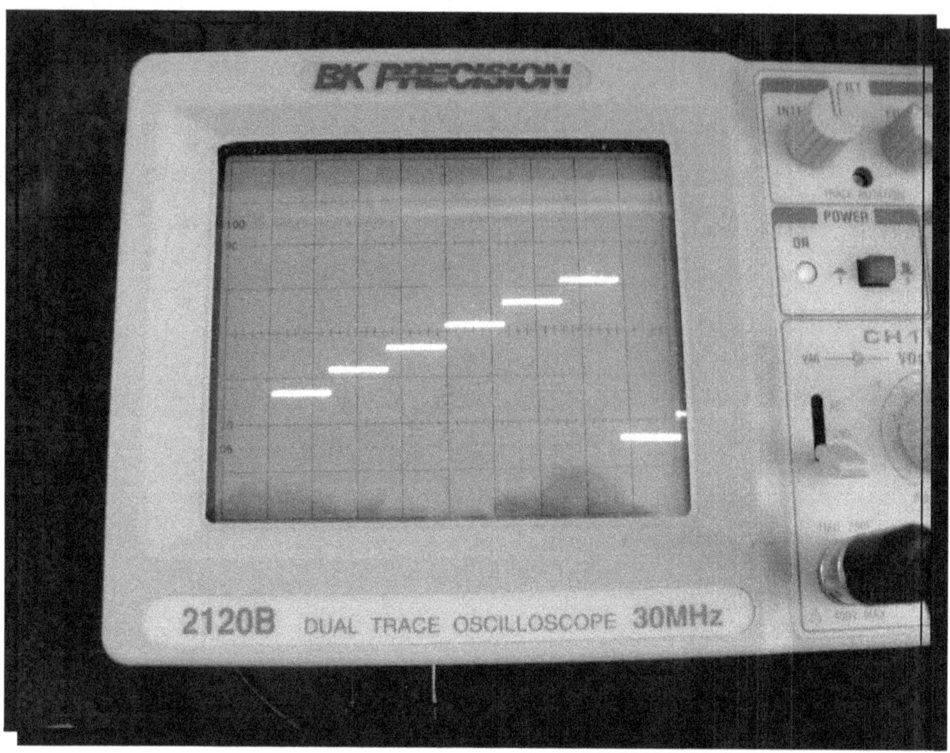

The step function shown above is a 50Hz signal of 4V p-p with an offset of 2.5V. With 10,000 samples it's likely that we will get a good mix of all the step values.

The step function is similar to a square wave in that it is composed of discrete voltage levels. When I first saw the plots of Figures 2-6 and 2-7, I said, "Of course." I think you will find this one easy to explain.

See how these regular signals produce predictable graphic plots?

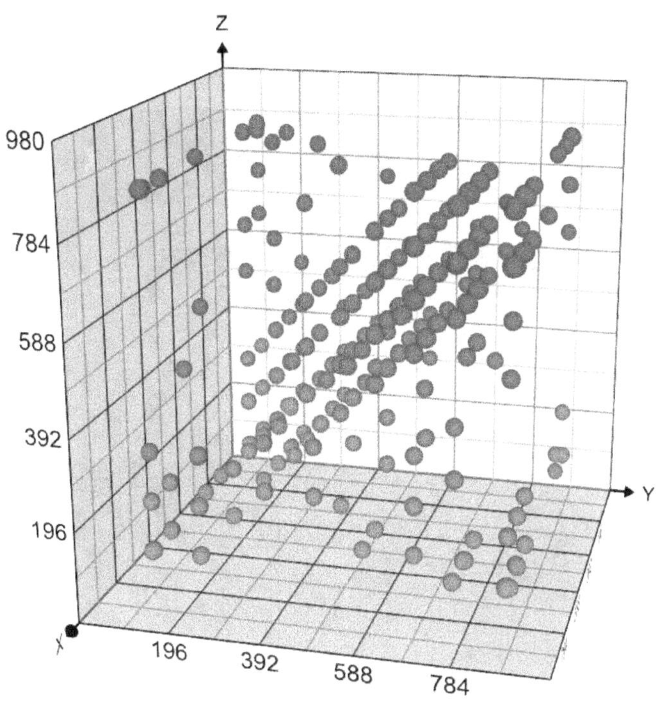

Figure 2-6. Step Function, View #1

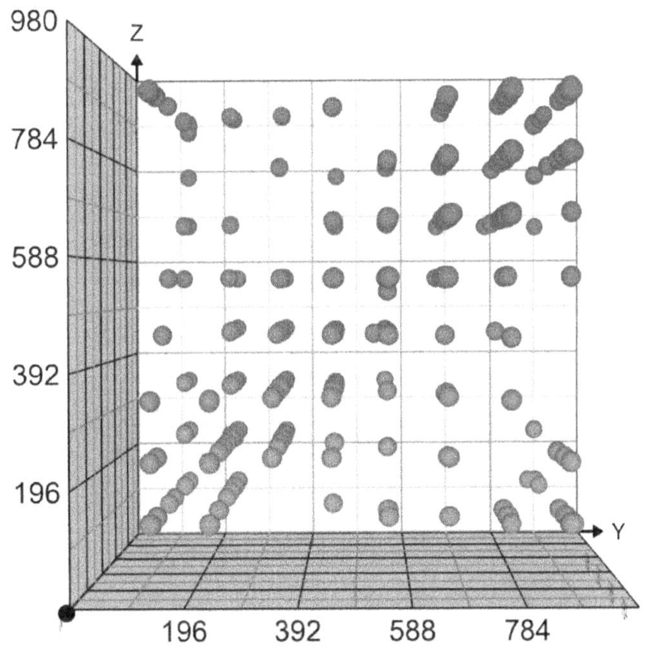

Figure 2-7. Step Function, View #2

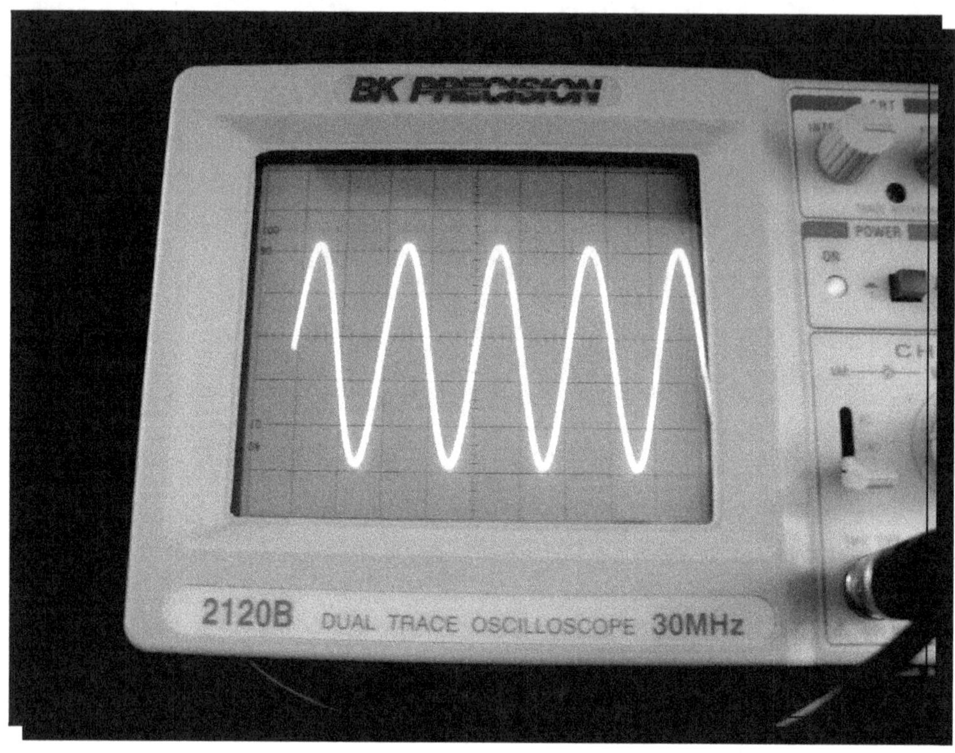

The sign wave shown above is simple, repetitive, and smooth. It contains no noise or overtone components. So, if we captured the signal at regular intervals and displayed the values graphically, what would you expect the plot to look like?

If our sample rate were the same as the frequency of the sine wave we would sample at exactly the same place every time as shown in Figure 2-8. Therefore, all of the samples would be the same number. This would result in only one dot on the screen. I expected that if our sample rate varied just a little bit we might see a smudge.

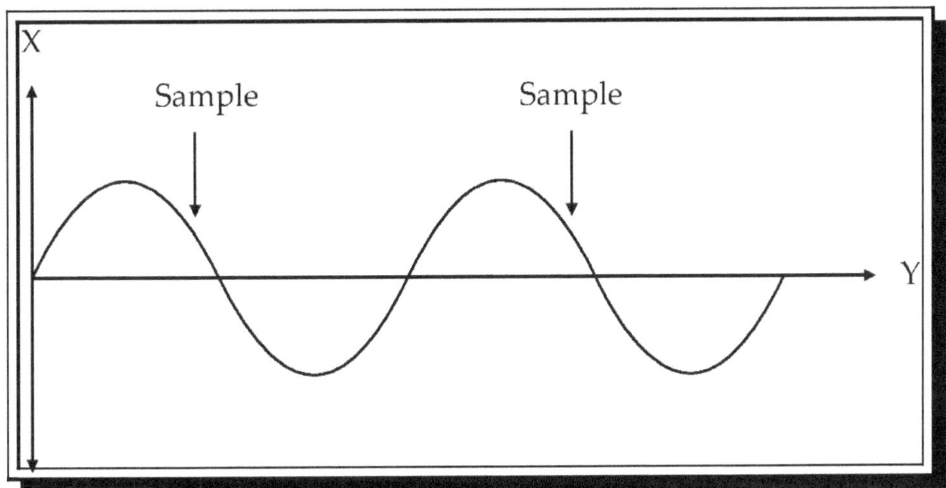

Figure 2-8. Consistent Samples

Our sampling rate while writing to a Class 10 SD card is about 50 samples per second, so I set the signal generator to 50Hz and got the plot shown in Figure 2-9. When I first saw this one I was completely blown away! It was nothing like I expected.

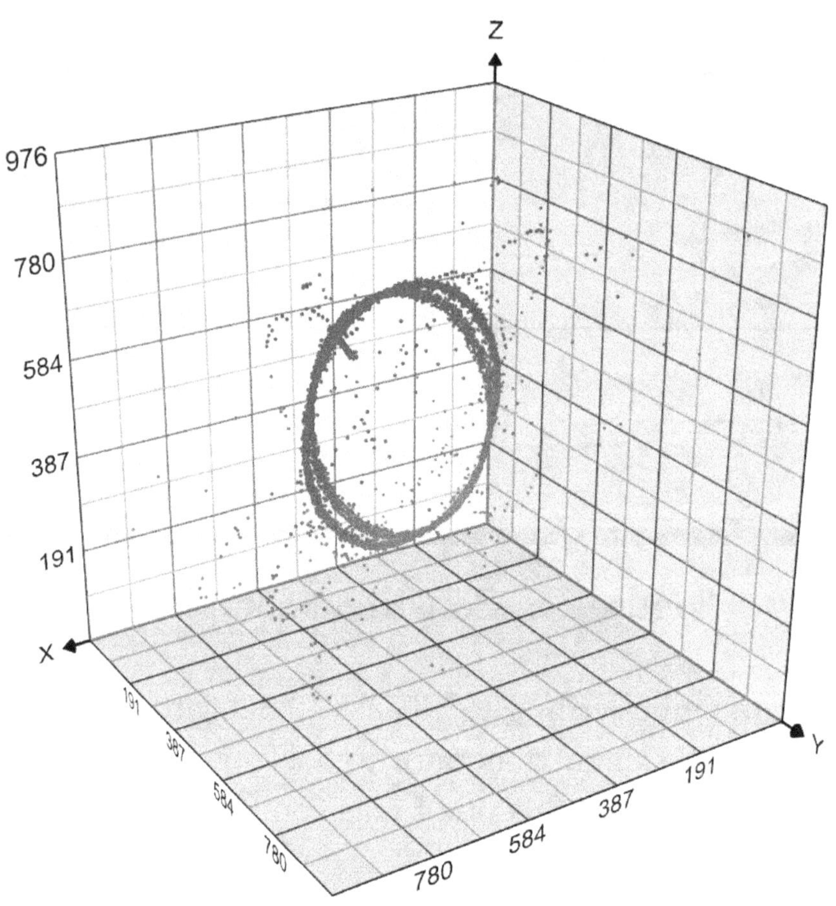

Figure 2-9. Sine Wave Plot (50Hz)

My initial thought was that our sampling rate was off by just a little bit, which would cause some "drift." So I captured several more datasets using different frequencies of sine wave. Each sample set consists of 10,000 samples. The amazing patterns of Figures 2-10 through 2-16 are not really all that surprising once you realize what's happening.

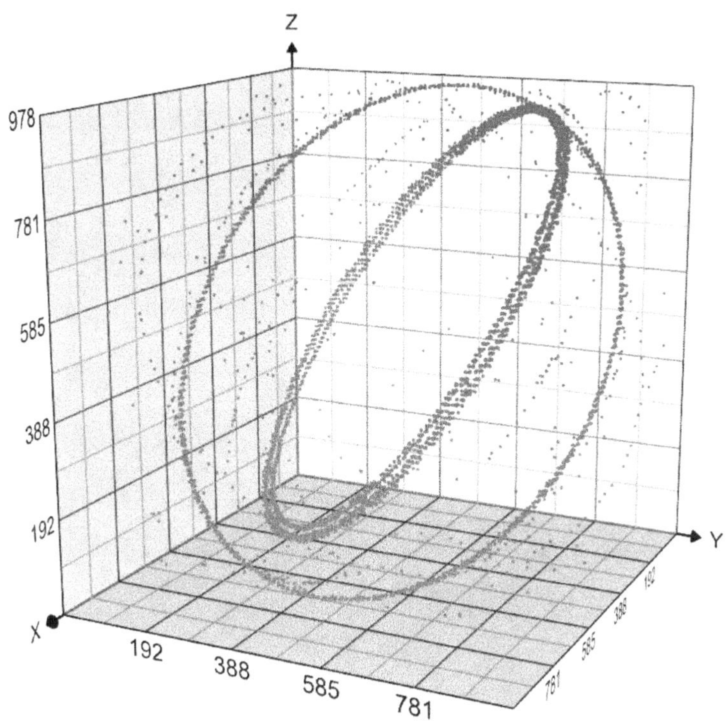

Figure 2-10. Sine Wave Plot, 60Hz

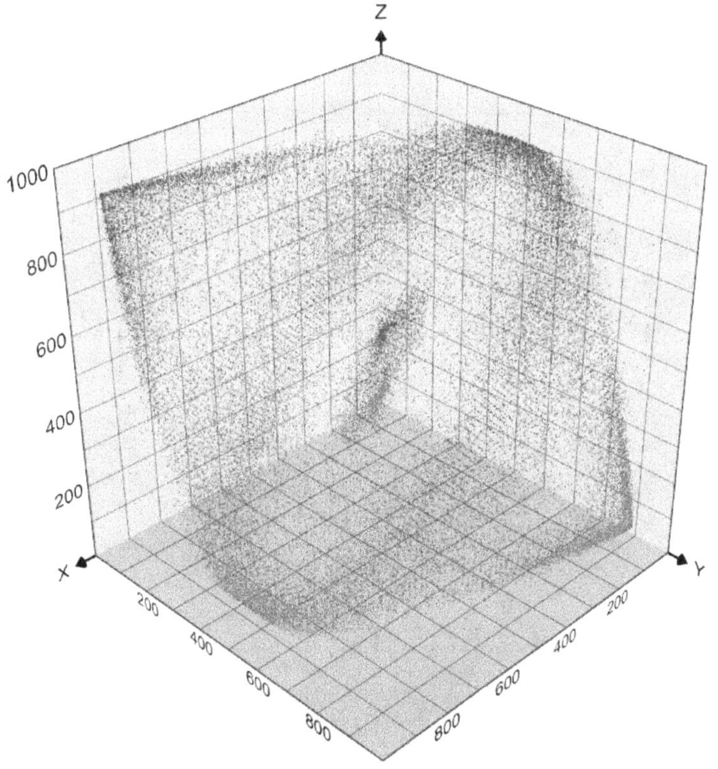

Figure 2-11. Sine Wave Plot, 70Hz

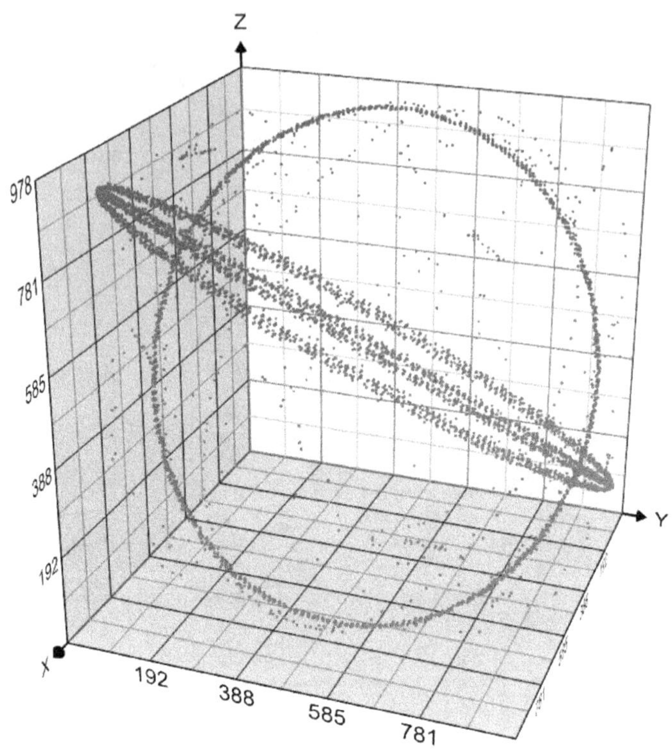

Figure 2-12. Sine Wave Plot, 80Hz

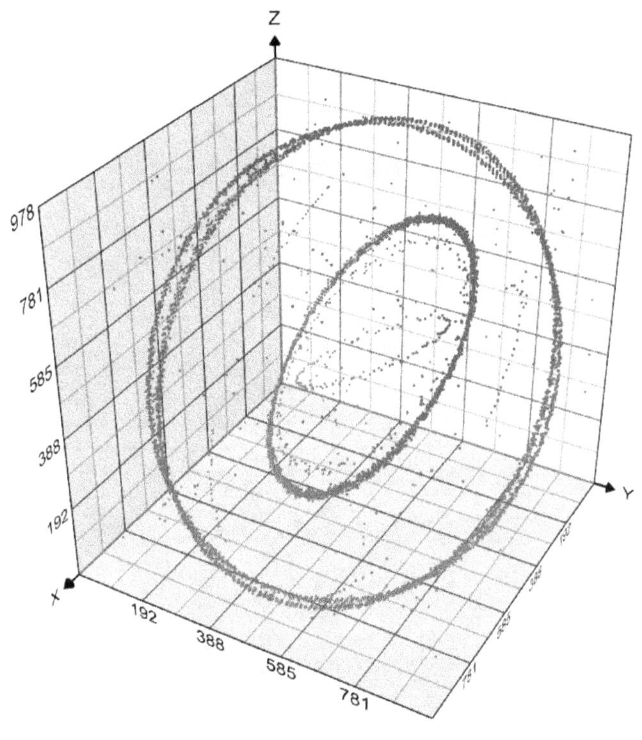

Figure 2-13. Sine Wave Plot, 90Hz

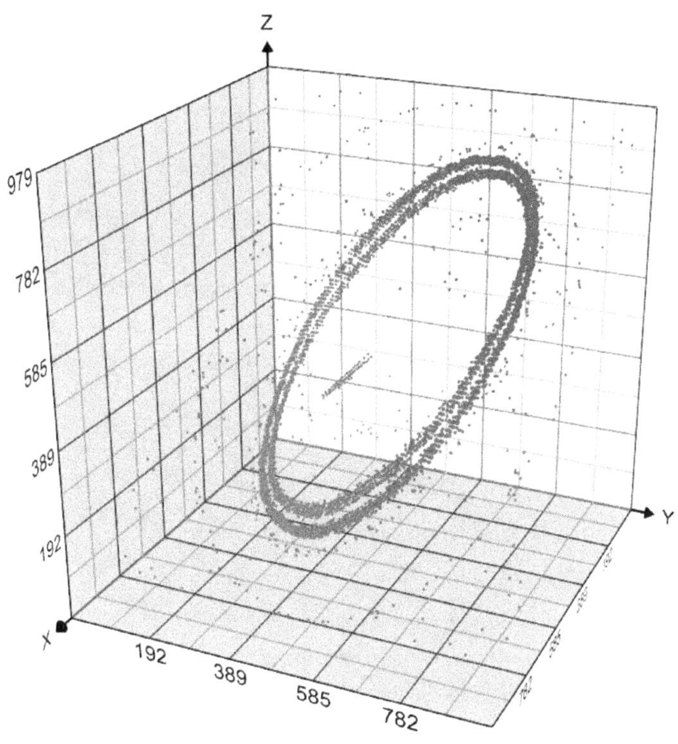

Figure 2-14. Sine Wave Plot, 100Hz

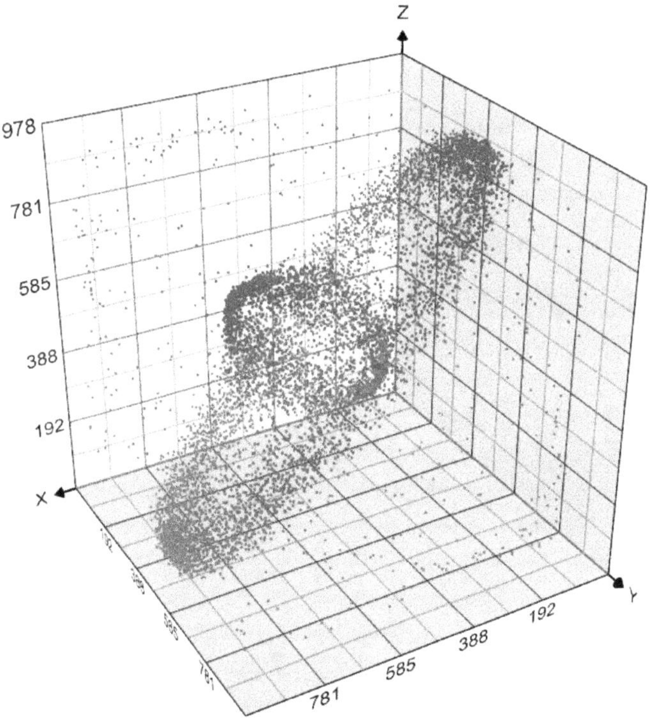

Figure 2-15. Sine Wave Plot, 1KHz

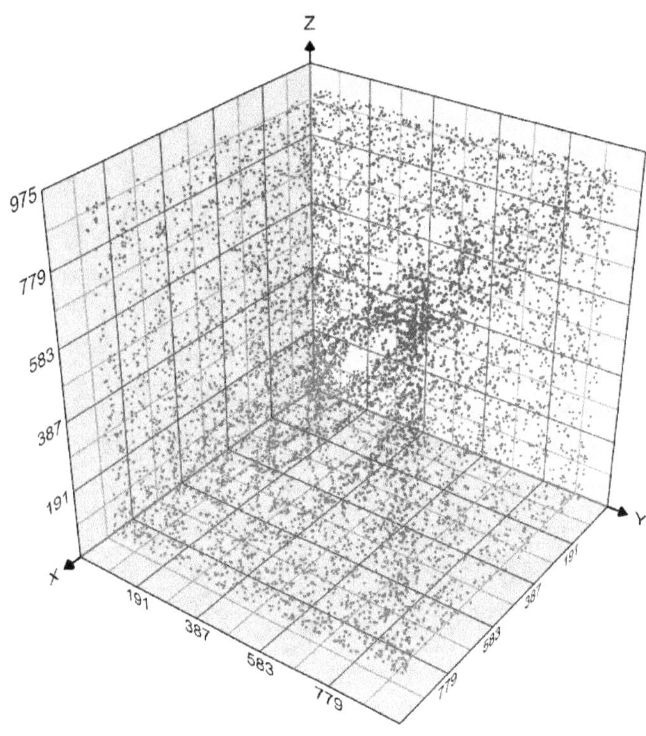

Figure 2-16. Sine Wave Plot, 10KHz

2.4.4 Triangular Wave

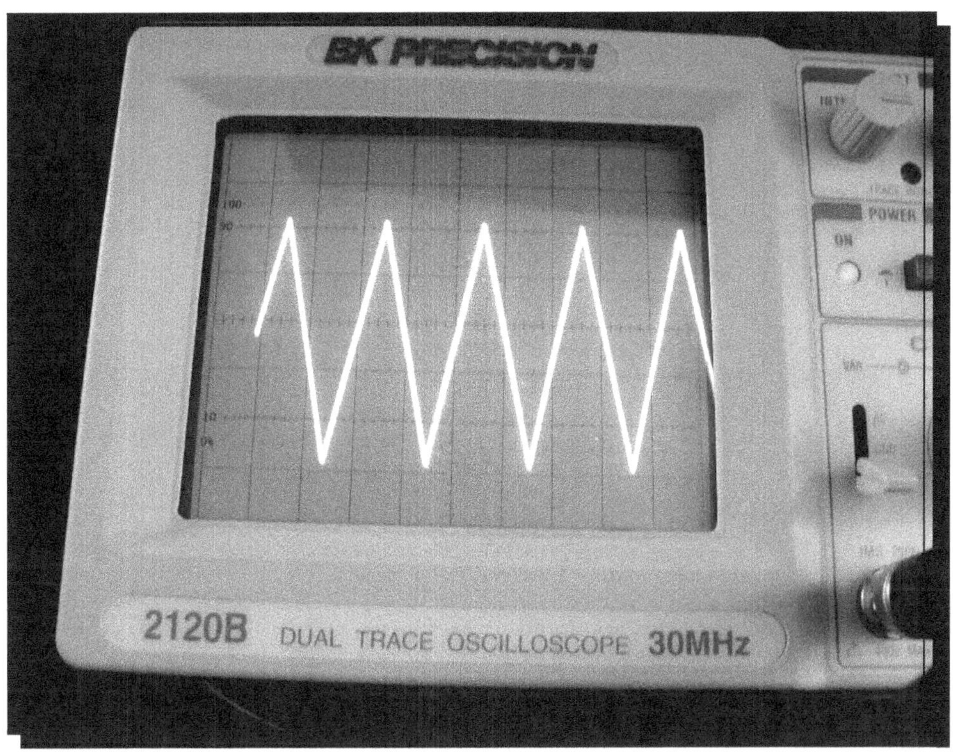

The triangular wave in many ways is similar to the sine wave, so we might expect similar plots. With 10,000 samples, we have the opportunity to capture virtually every value between its low and high points, but the relationships between the captured values are different from those of the sine wave. Figures 2-17 through 2-24 show plots taken at the same frequencies as the sine wave plots shown above. Here again, it makes sense that sampling regular, repeating signals should produce clear patterns in the plots.

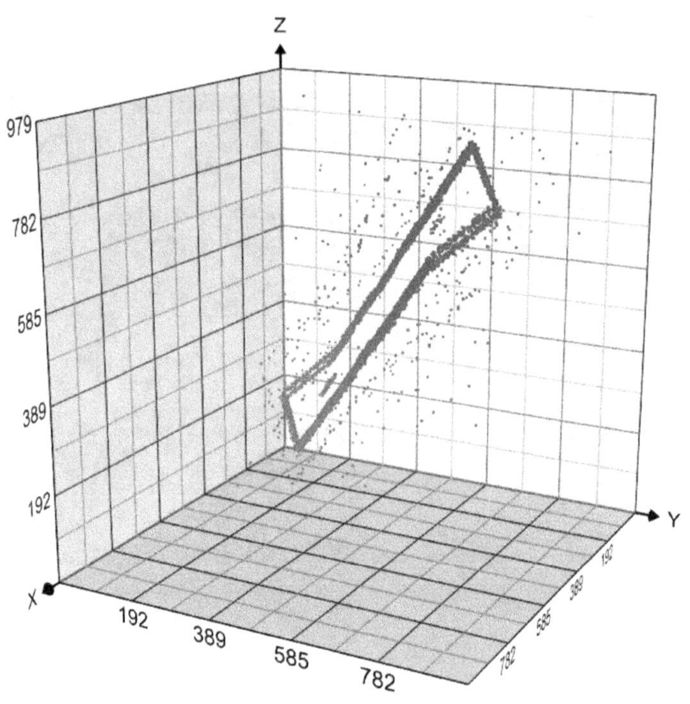

Figure 2-17. Triangular Wave, 50Hz

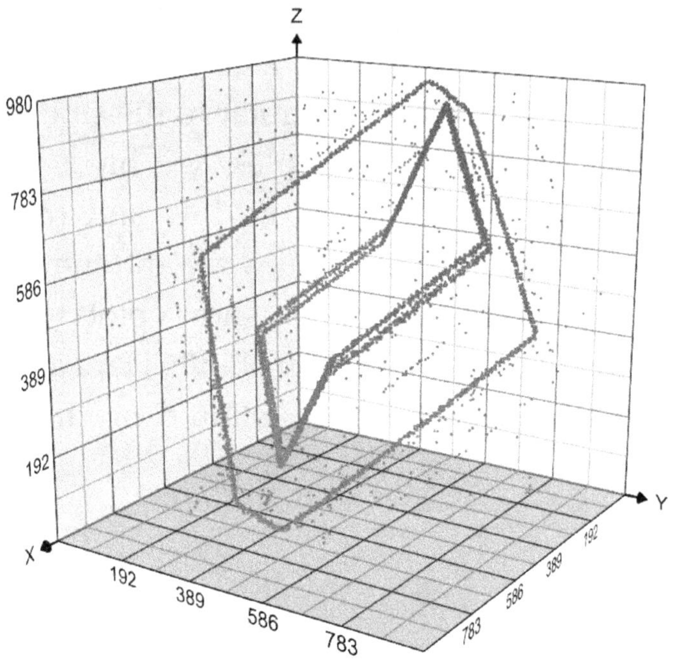

Figure 2-18. Triangular Wave, 60Hz

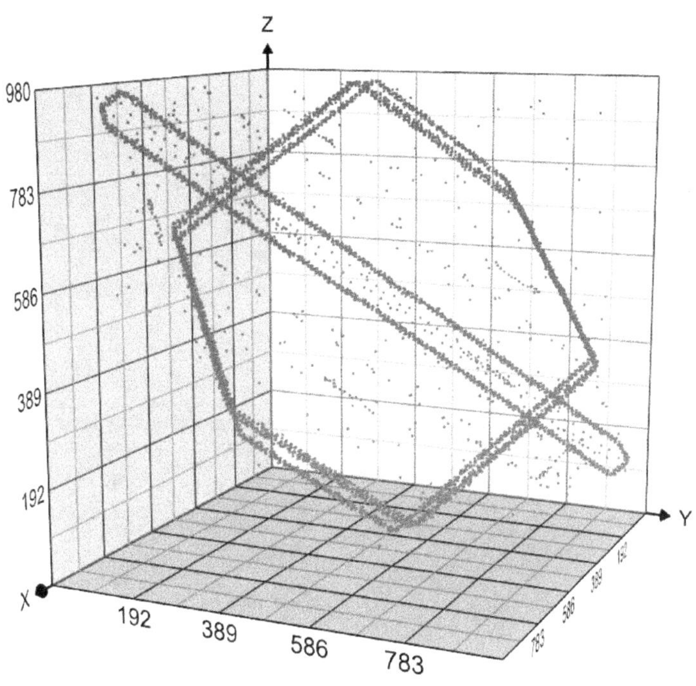

Figure 2-19. Triangular Wave, 70Hz

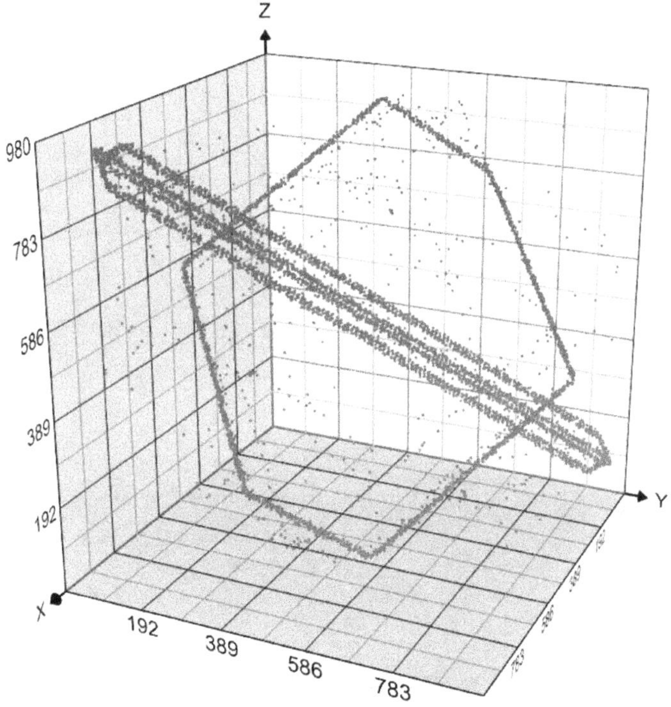

Figure 2-20. Triangular Wave, 80Hz

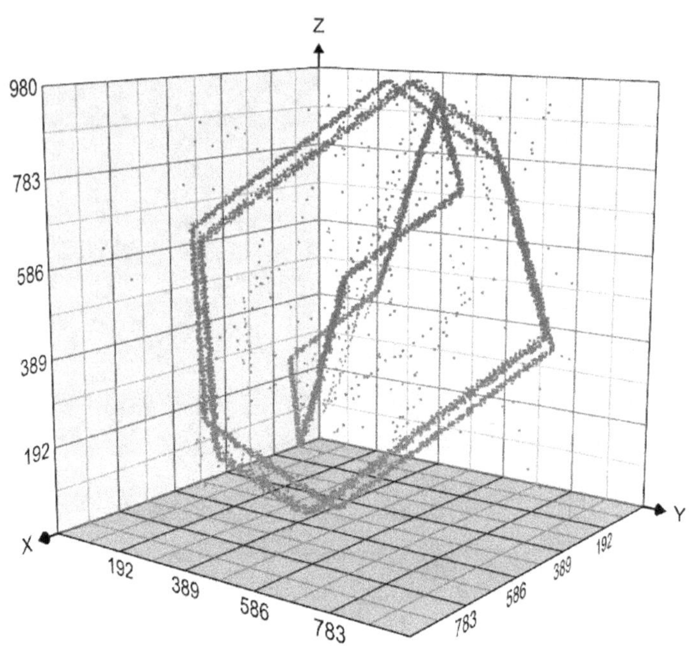

Figure 2-21. Triangular Wave, 90Hz

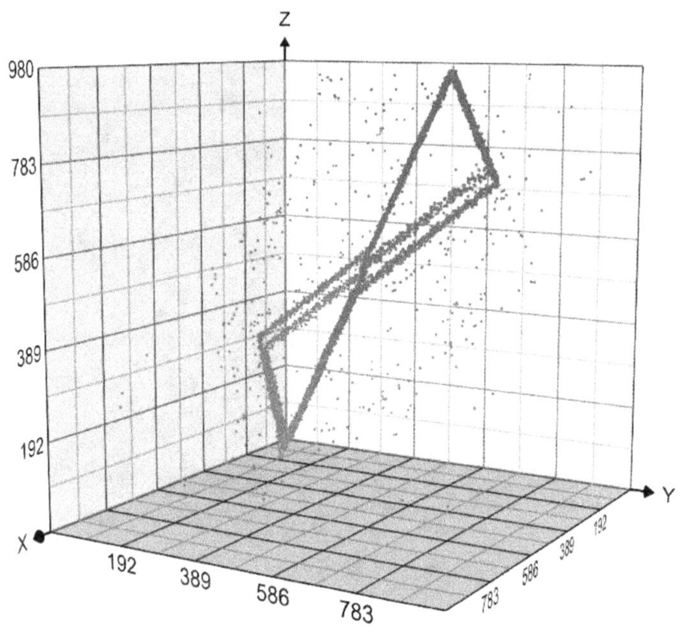

Figure 2-22. Triangular Wave, 100Hz

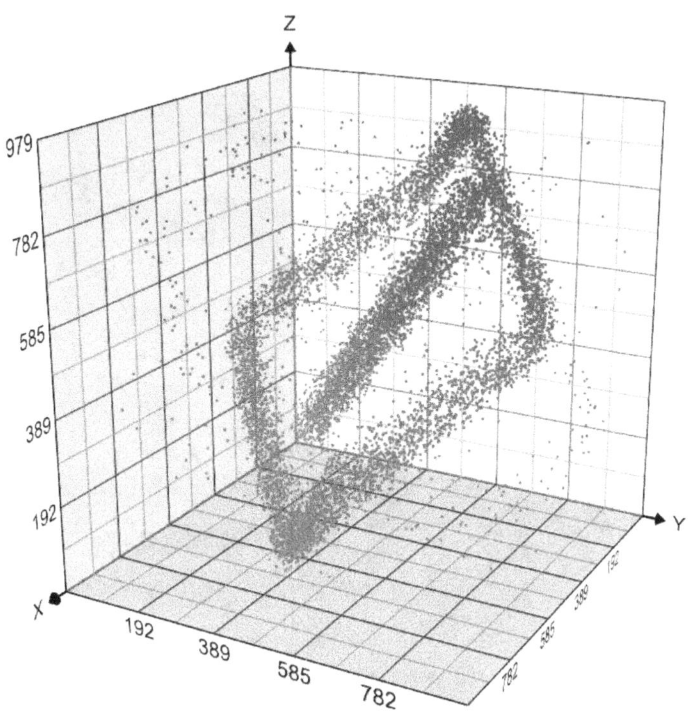

Figure 2-23. Triangular Wave, 1KHz

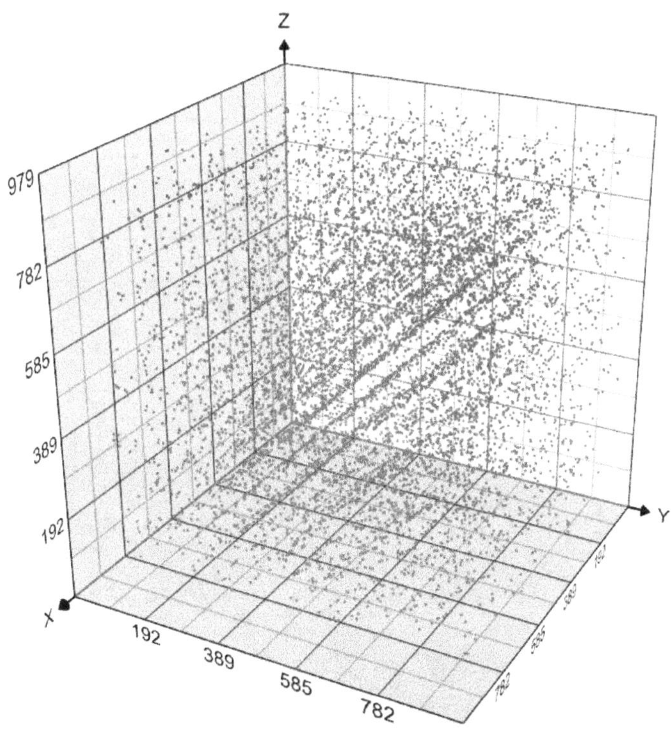

Figure 2-24. Triangular Wave, 10KHz

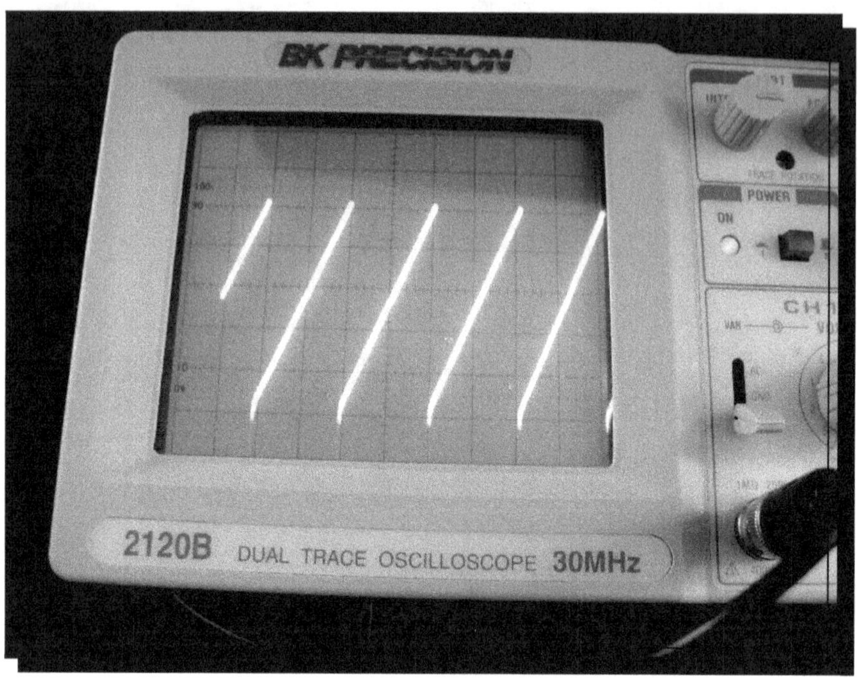

In Figures 2-25 and 2-26 we have a quick look at a 10KHz ramp function sampled at 50 samples per second. Again, this is a pretty simple, repetitive signal. Can you anticipate what the plot will look like?

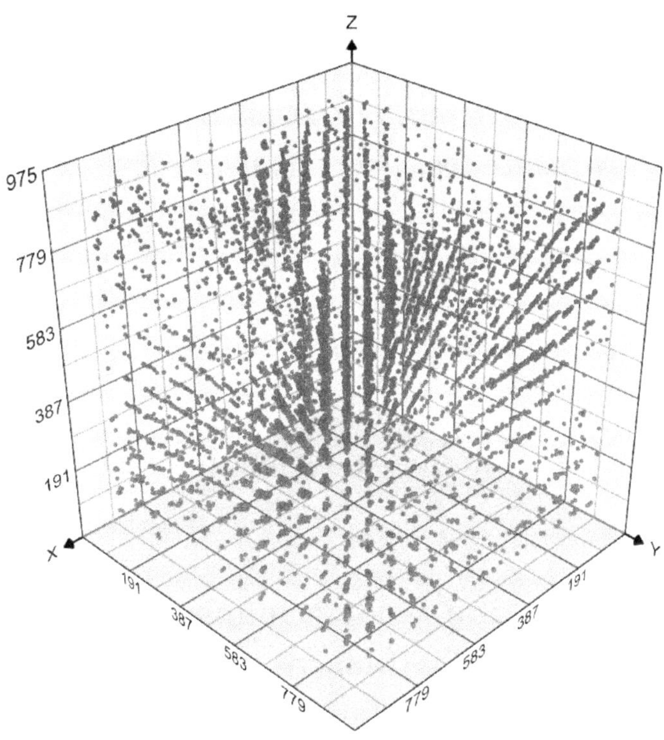

Figure 2-25. Ramp Function, View #1

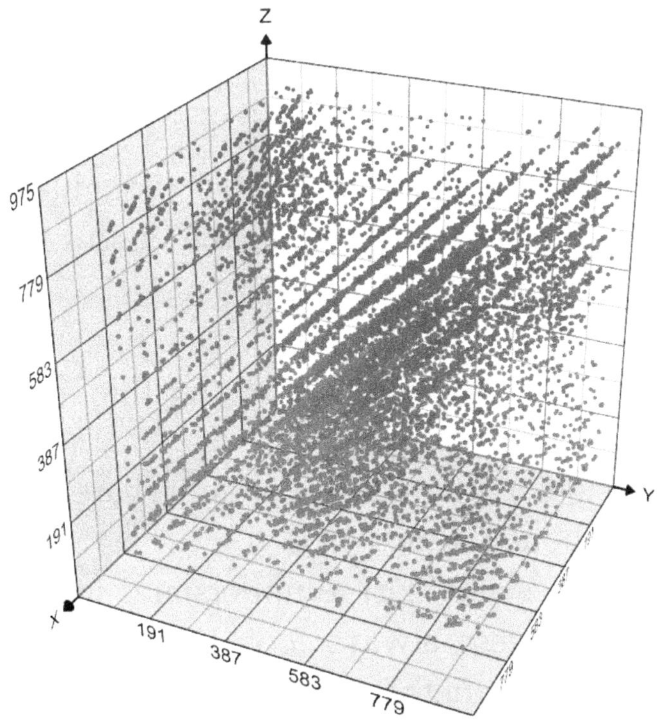

Figure 2-26. Ramp Function, View #2

2.4.6 Random Numbers

My personal theory is that there is no such thing as "random" but we won't get into that here.

Figure 2-27 is a 2-D plot of a random number set, and Figure 2-28 is the same dataset displayed in 3-D. If all the numbers are truly random, there can be no detectable pattern, right? The human mind has an amazing capacity to detect patterns! In ancient times our survival depended on it (if you drive in Phoenix, Arizona it probably still does). In Appendix E we will discuss the BASIC routine used to generate our random number matrix.

When I first saw the plot of Figure 2-27, I thought it looked like cow leather. That got me to thinking that the discovery of patterns (or randomness) in nature might work both ways:

1. We discover a pattern where we didn't think one existed and we learn something about nature.
2. We see an obvious pattern and wonder where it came from. Again, we learn more about nature.
3. We see randomness and start to understand what randomness looks like. Does randomness always look the same or are some things "more random" than others?

Many of the experiments in this book capture information from natural phenomena that, at first, seem random but the plots show distinct patterns. In this case I don't see any patterns whatsoever.

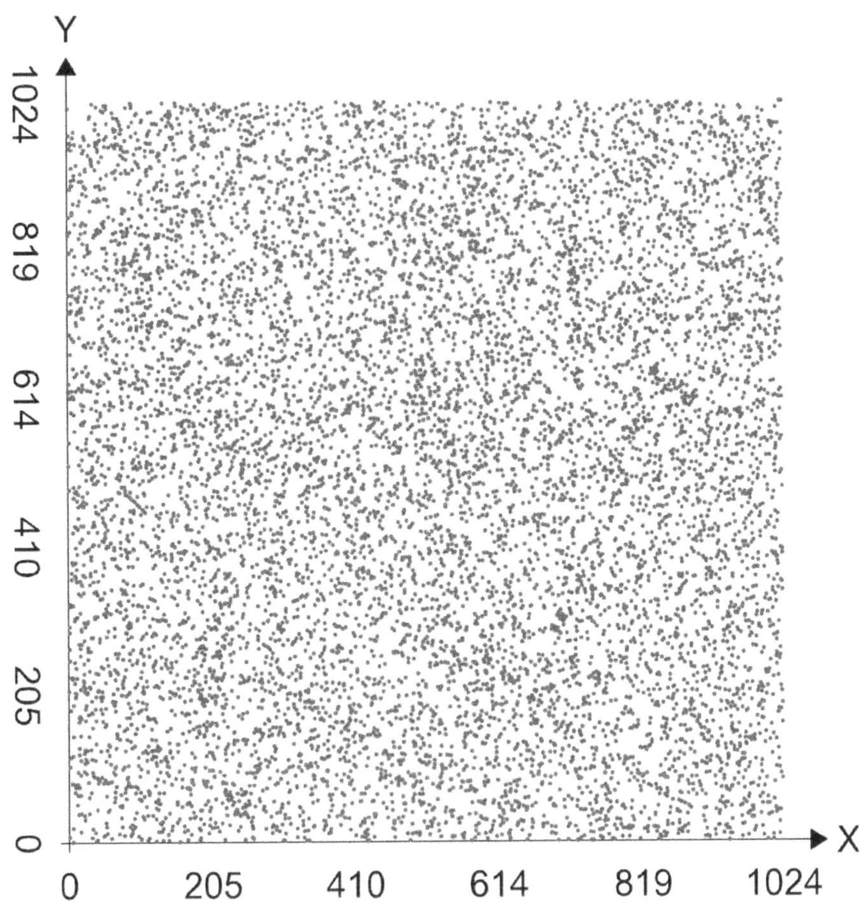

Figure 2-27. Random Numbers, 2-D Plot

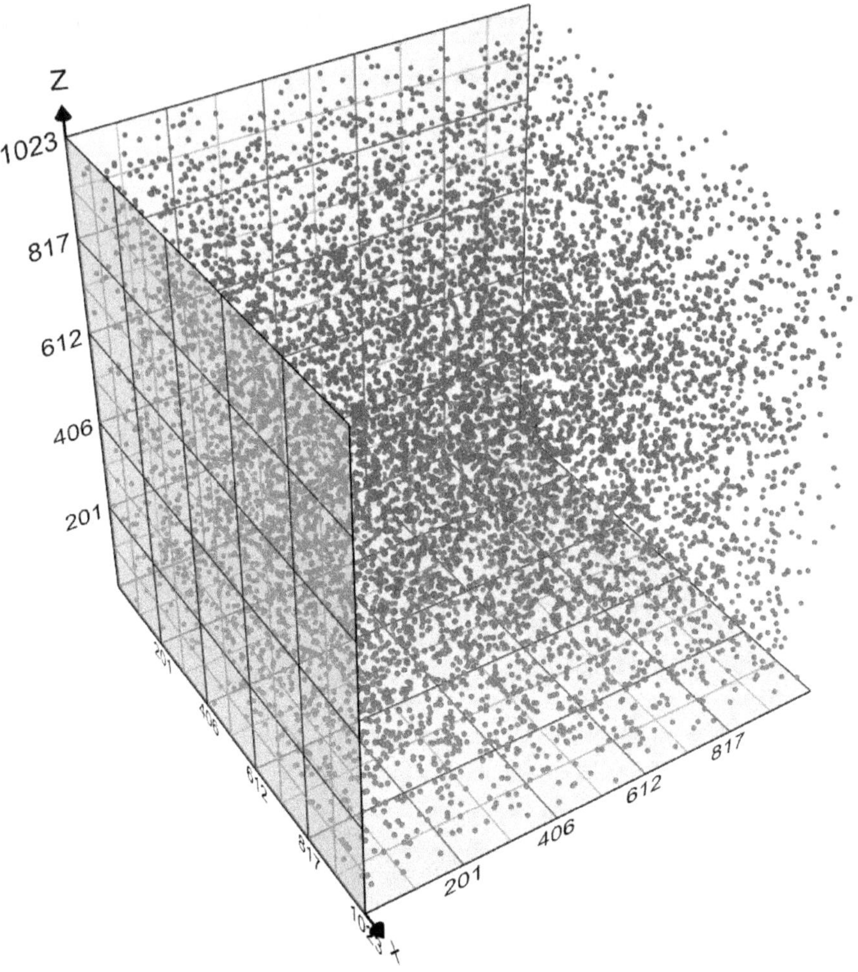

Figure 2-28. Random Numbers, 3-D Plot

Box fans are great! They can help cut your cooling cost during the summer and they have such a relaxing sound.

What is that sound? Ocean waves are relaxing too, but they have a fairly predictable pattern. Can you hear a pattern in a box fan? After all, the motor runs on 60-cycle power (50-cycle power in Europe). Well, let's have a look. For the following plot I recorded the sound of a box fan and then used a microphone shield on the Arduino A0 analog port to sample it.

In Figures 2-29 and 2-30 you can see that, in three dimensions, it looks like a fuzzy ball because most of the energy is contained within certain frequencies. See how closely the sound of a box fan resembles white noise shown in the next section?

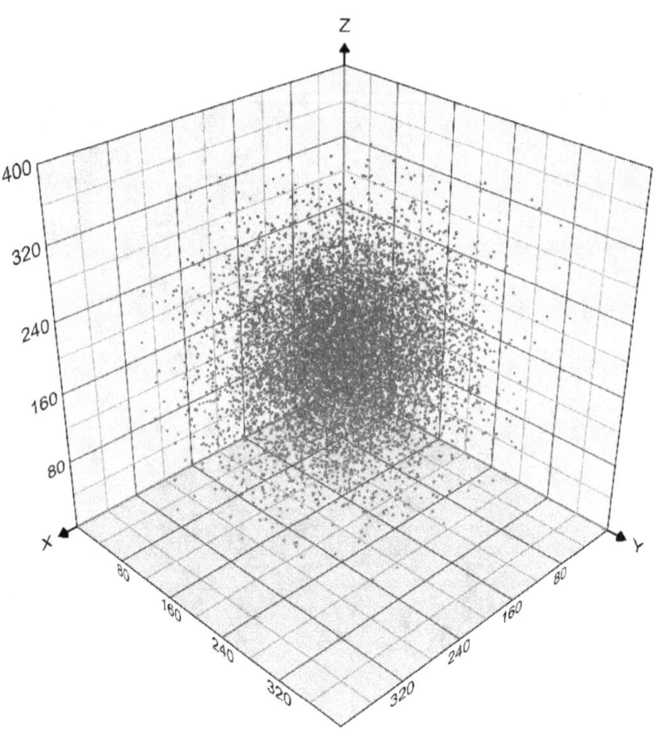

Figure 2-29. Box Fan, View #1

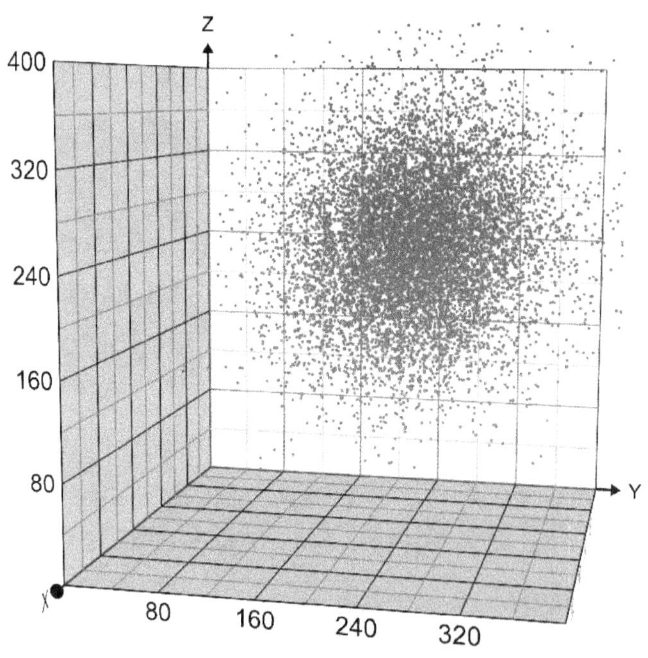

Figure 2-30. Box Fan, View #2

2.4.8 White Noise

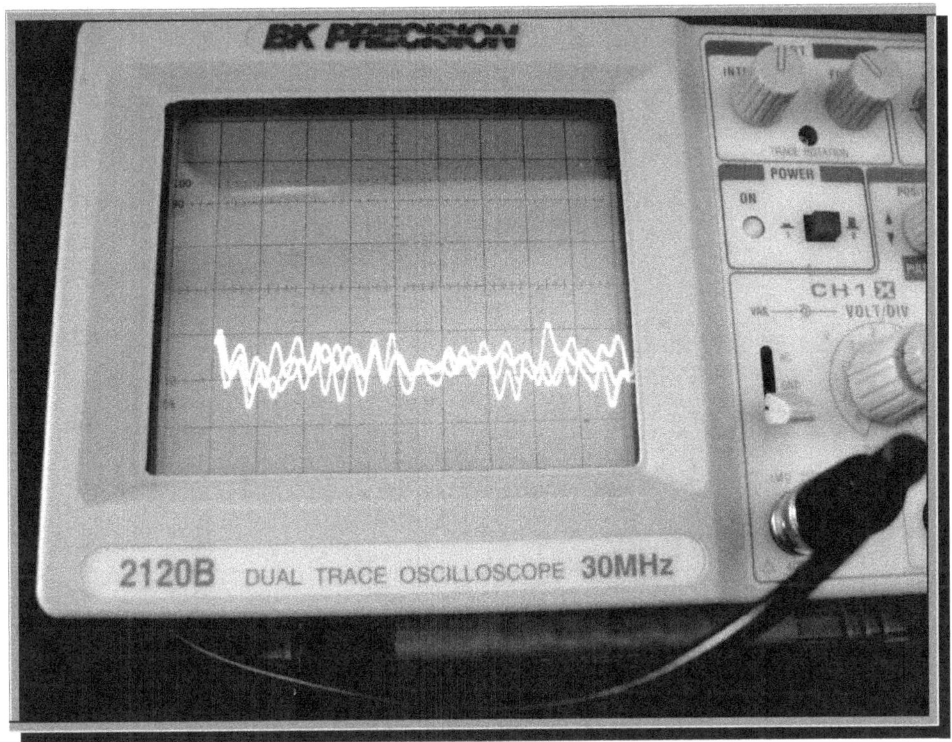

I don't sleep very well at night, so I like to have some kind of sounds to cover up background noise and help me relax. My little "Sound Spa" is great for that! White noise is not completely random because it has a sonic center. Why? Well, because we want to hear it, so it needs to be within the human hearing range. But we don't want to be distracted by recurring patterns.

If you can read the buttons on the Sound Spa in Figure 2-31 you will see that it is capable of producing white noise, rain, summer night, brook, ocean, and thunder. They may not be perfect, but the sounds are relaxing. I used it to record the white noise pattern for Figures 2-32 and 2-33.

Figure 2-31. Sound Spa

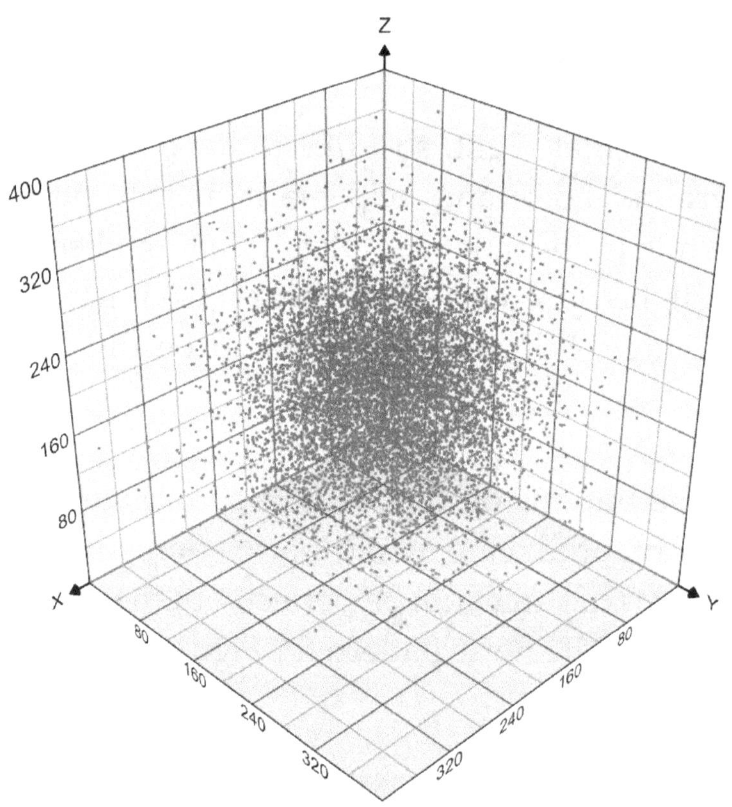

Figure 2-32. White Noise, View #1

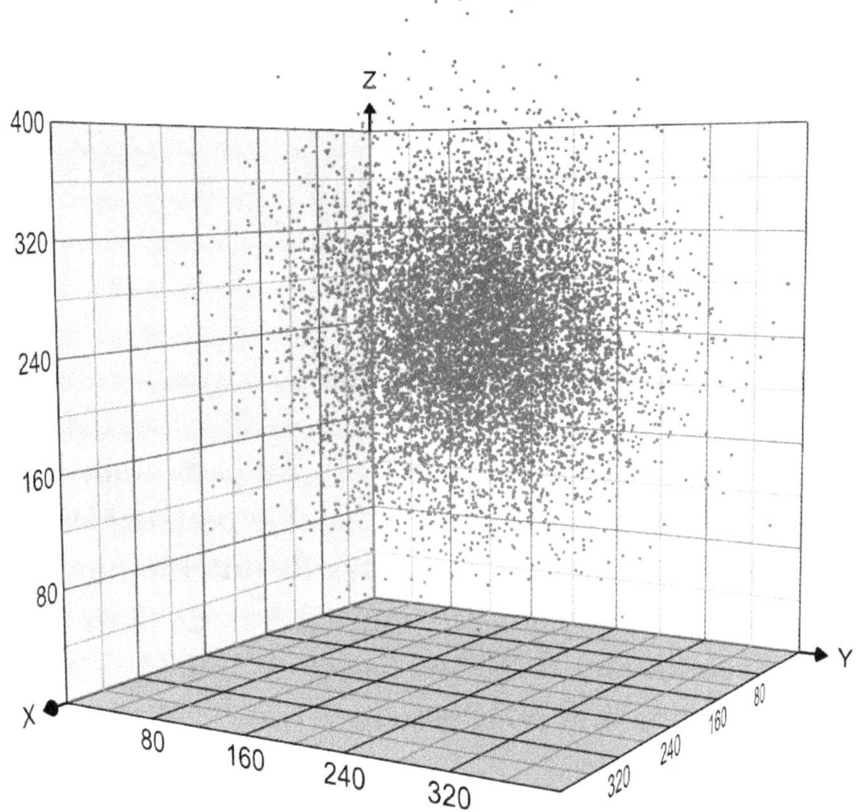

Figure 2-33. White Noise, View #2

A dripping faucet can be very annoying, and it can inflate your water bill, but do these annoying drops have a predictable pattern? We'll spend more time on this fascinating topic in Chapter 3, but for now, here are two amazing plots of a dripping faucet. Figure 2-34 was derived by capturing 50 samples per second. Figure 2-35 is based on the same audio recording, but it is a plot of the time intervals between drops. I had the drip rate set so that it sounded random to me.

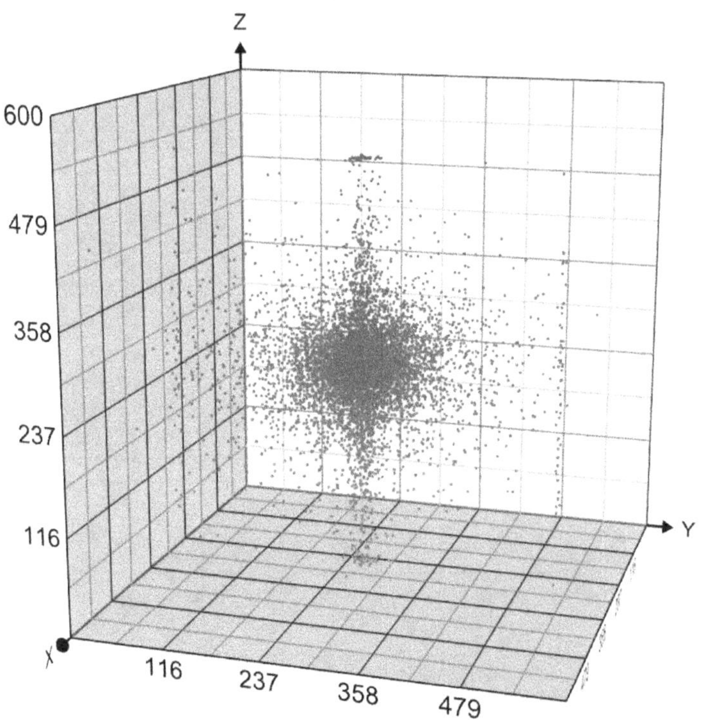

Figure 2-34. Dripping Faucet, Sampled at Regular Intervals

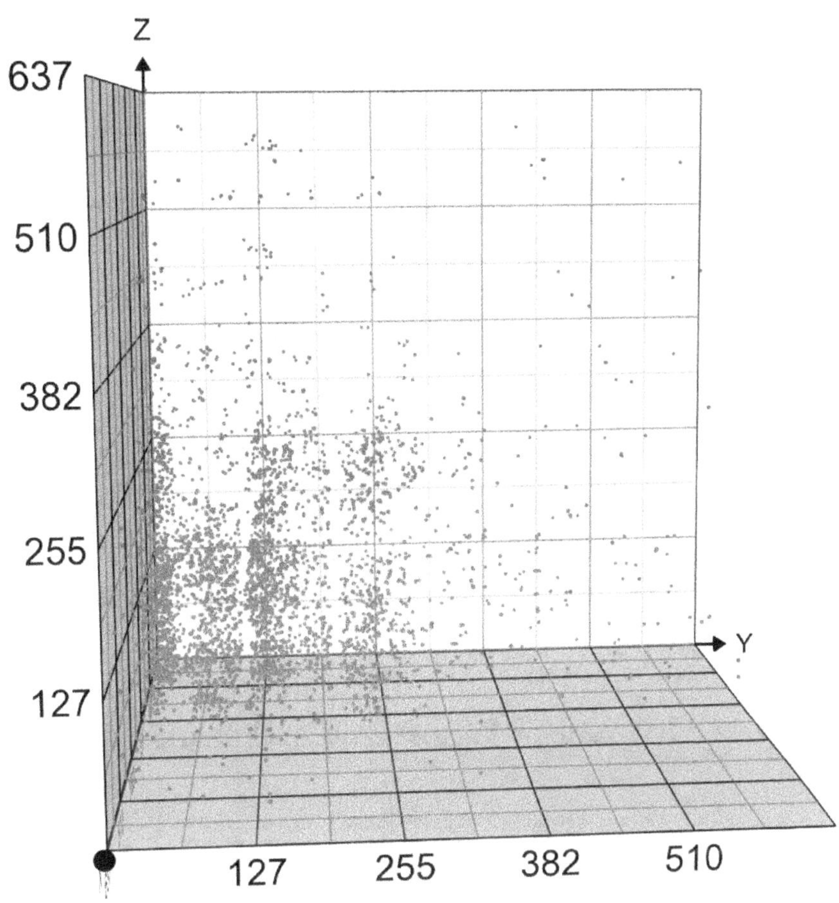

Figure 2-35. Dripping Faucet, Interrupt Based Approach

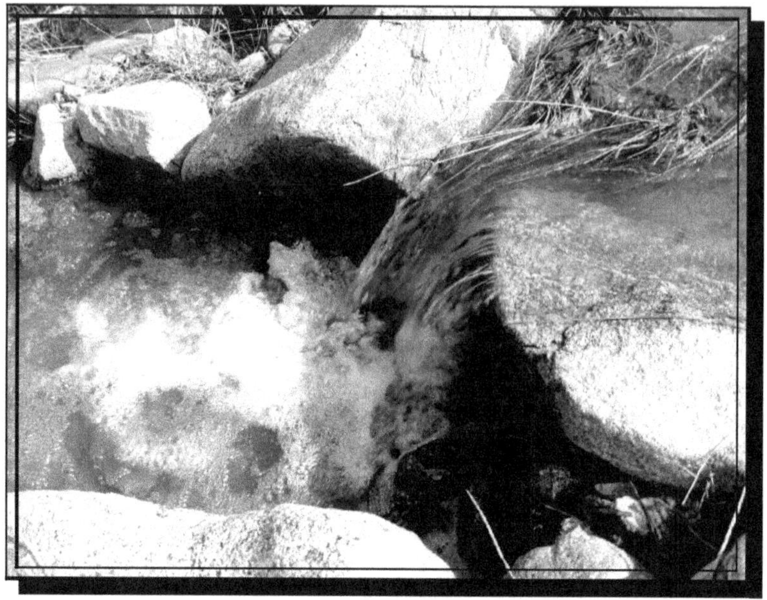

Waterfalls have such a complex sound! Sometimes I think that I hear some repeating patterns. Do I really? Figure 2-36 makes me think otherwise.

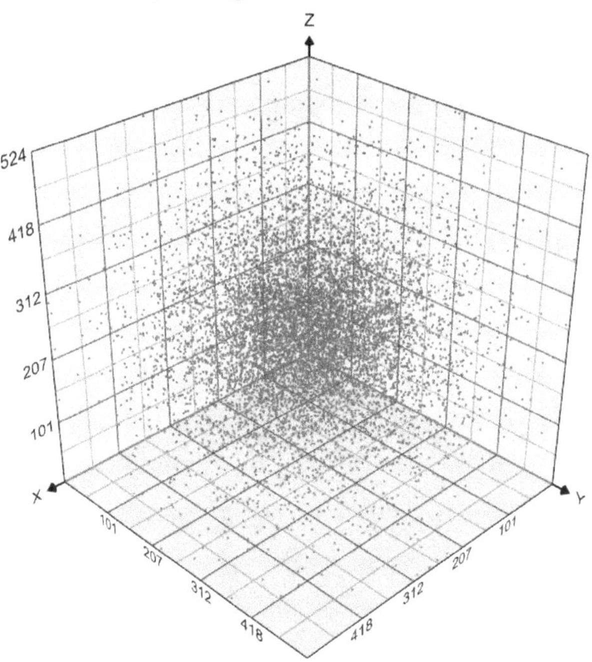

Figure 2-36. Waterfall Plot

2.4.11 Wind

There are several different ways that we can capture information about the wind. We can't see the wind directly but we can see its effect. The voltages for Figure 2-37 came from a photoresistor setting in the shade of a tree branch that was being blown back and forth in the wind.

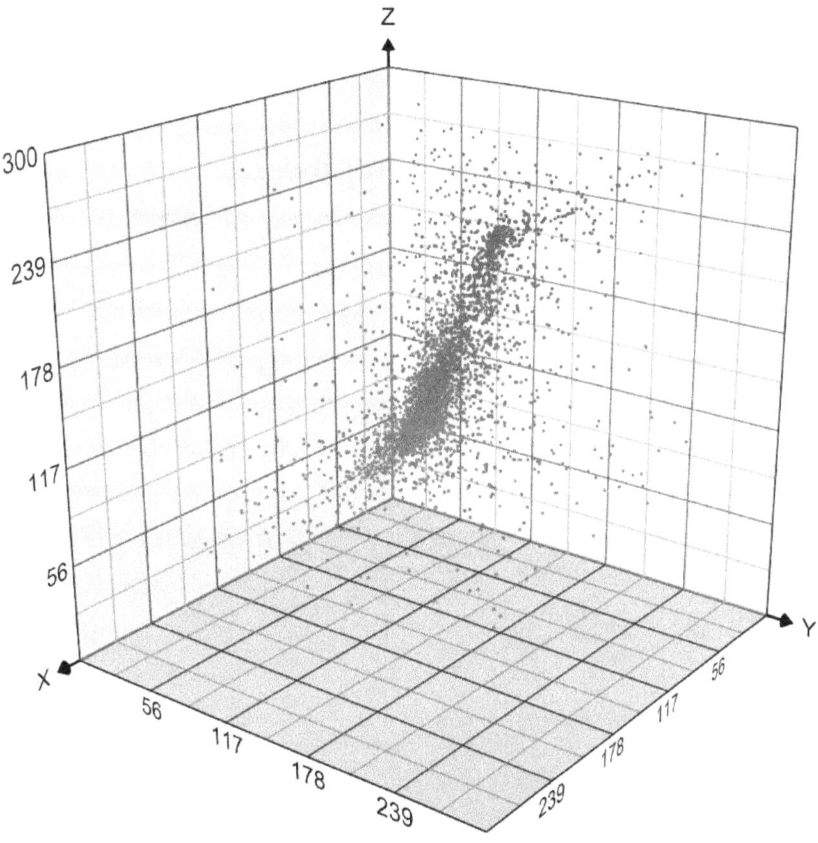

Figure 2-37. Blowing in the Wind

2.5 How to Proceed?

In this chapter we have had a quick look at plots ranging from simple and repetitive to random, to chaotic. In Chapter 3 we will start an exciting journey of exploration. We will study a variety of natural events. They involve movement, sound and light. Some happen very quickly and others take more time. For an analog event like a tree branch moving in the wind we will measure the movement directly using an accelerometer and we will also use a photoresistor to measure the movement of its shadow.

So, for each of these experiments, we will need to design an experiment and answer the following questions:

1. What information do we hope to capture?
2. What type of sensors do we need in order to capture the data accurately? Do we need to make special jigs to hold the sensors?
3. How can we put the data in a form that is useable?
4. What type of analysis does it require?
5. How will we present the results graphically?
6. How will we know if we have discovered anything?

Chapter 3: It Began with a Dripping Faucet

3.1 Childhood Memories

When I was a kid we didn't have a lot of money. We weren't really poor, but we couldn't afford to hire things done for us. My dad was very versatile and was able to fix almost anything. The exception? Pluming. In those days when you wanted to stop the faucet from dripping you just squeezed the handle tighter. When you do that you eventually reach a point where the washer is flattened and more squeezing doesn't help that much. So, I've heard my share of dripping faucets.

Maybe you haven't thought much about dripping faucets, but it's a pretty complex affair. Water tends to build up on the lip of the faucet and eventually a drop falls off. But there is more to it than that. With new water coming in, the drop tends to oscillate up and down until there is enough weight to break the cohesive forces of the drop, and it lets go (usually at the bottom of an oscillation). Who would have thought that all that stuff is going on for each drop!

A dripping faucet seems to operate in three different modes:

Mode 1: At a very slow rate the drops are pretty steady.

Mode 2: A little faster and they seem to become random, and then
Mode 3: At a high flow rate it turns into a steady stream.

The situation we are interested in is Mode 2. I call it the "chaotic" mode. Here's where the drops seem to be random or at least unpredictable. How could such a complex event as this contain any patterns or attractors at all? Well, this is our first experiment.

Visit my website at rickmckeon.com/mcu.html for some interesting videos on this topic.

3.2 Capturing and Displaying the Data

The first thing we need to do is design an experiment to capture information from the system and put it in a form that is useful for analysis. For any system, that means capturing the event (sound, light, pressure, movement, etc.) and converting it into numbers. Then we need to present those numbers in a way that might reveal any hidden patterns.

Figure 3-1 shows the overall plan, and Figure 3-2 shows the setup for capture. You may want to simplify this process a little bit (maybe eliminate the audio recorder and capture directly with the Arduino) but this is the procedure I followed:

1. Capture the sound of the dripping faucet as an mp3 file using an audio recorder.
2. Transfer the audio file to the computer so that you can play it back through the computer speakers with volume control.
3. Sample the audio file with a microphone shield on the Arduino, and log those numbers to a text file called "datalog.txt" on the SD card.
4. Remove the SD card from the Arduino SD shield and transfer the datalog.txt to the computer.

5. Write a BASIC program in QB64 that will read the numbers from datafile.txt and convert them to a three-column comma separated variable (csv) file.

6. Import this file to your favorite display software. I used *Graphing Calculator 3D* to do the visualization. This software is completely GUI based with no coding required, so it is intuitive and easy to use. Of course you can use any graphing program you are familiar with. I have used GNU Octave to produce the same plots, but in my opinion, this program is quicker and easier. There is a free demo version available, but to do anything useful you need to purchase at least the Standard version.

7. Then the real fun begins! Look for patterns in the graphical displays and see if you can understand where these patterns came from.

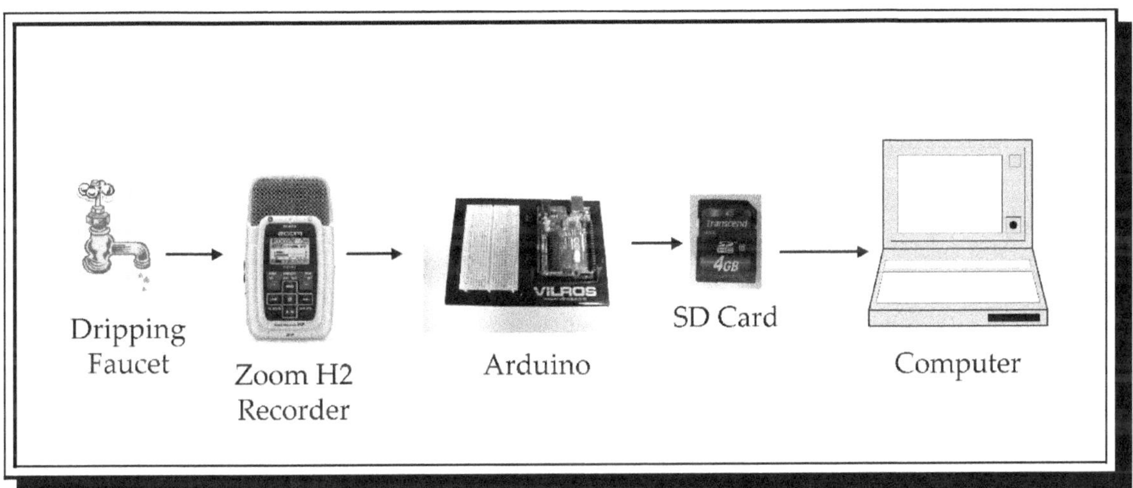

Figure 3-1. Capturing the Dripping Faucet

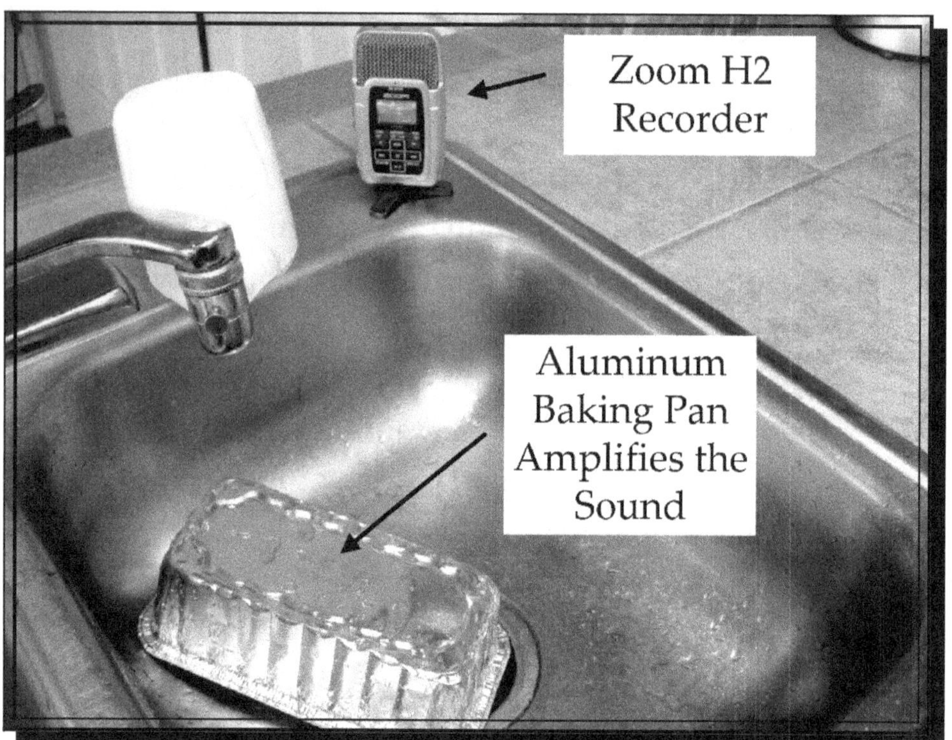

Figure 3-2. Recording the Dripping Faucet

We could capture the dripping faucet in other ways, like having the drops interrupt an LED/Photodiode pair or fall on a pressure sensor, but for this project I chose to record the sound of the drops.

3.2.1 Arduino as Data Logger

We are going to use the Arduino UNO to log the captured data. It has some on-board storage, but we will use an SD card "shield" to increase its storage capacity. For each of these projects we will be capturing 10,000 samples.

The beauty of the Arduino is that it can be used at home or in the field to capture and store information because it:

1. Stores the program in non-volatile memory.
2. Starts running the program upon power up, and
3. Can be powered via the USB connector or from a single 9V battery.

Figures 3-3 and 3-4 show the simple arrangement used to capture data with the Arduino. I recorded the sound of the dripping faucet with a Zoom H2 recorder and transferred it to my computer as an mp3 audio file. Then I played the audio file through the computer's speakers. Playing the audio file back via the computer speakers allowed me to adjust the volume so it was in a good range for the Arduino to capture. We are using a microphone sensor on the breadboard that feeds the signal to analog port A0 of the Arduino. The microphone is an Adafruit Electret Microphone Amplifier MAX9814.

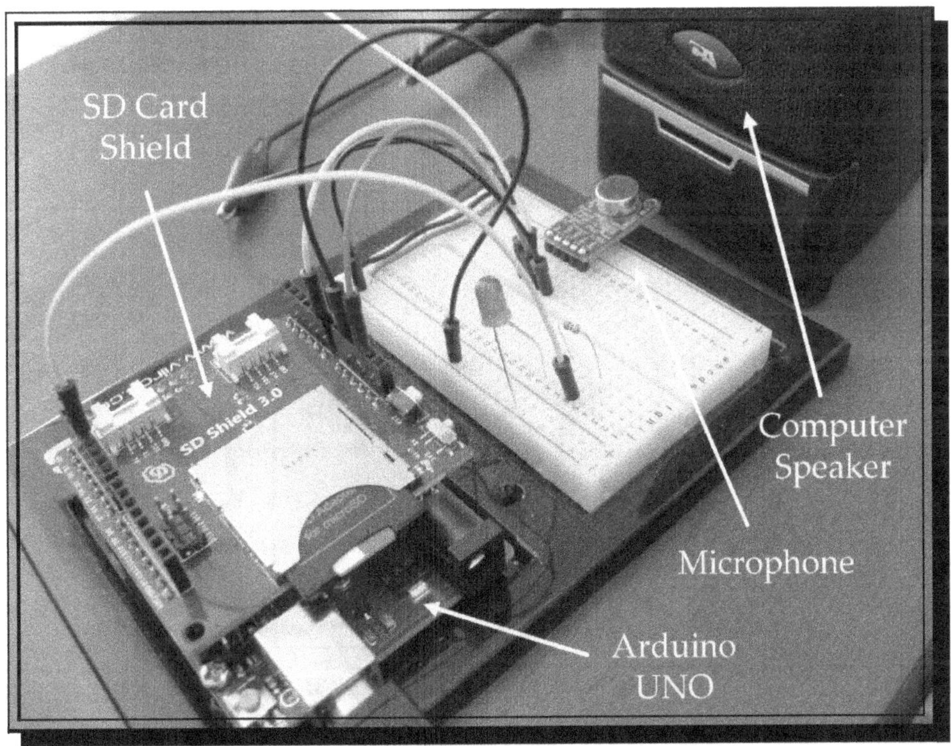

Figure 3-3. Equipment Setup

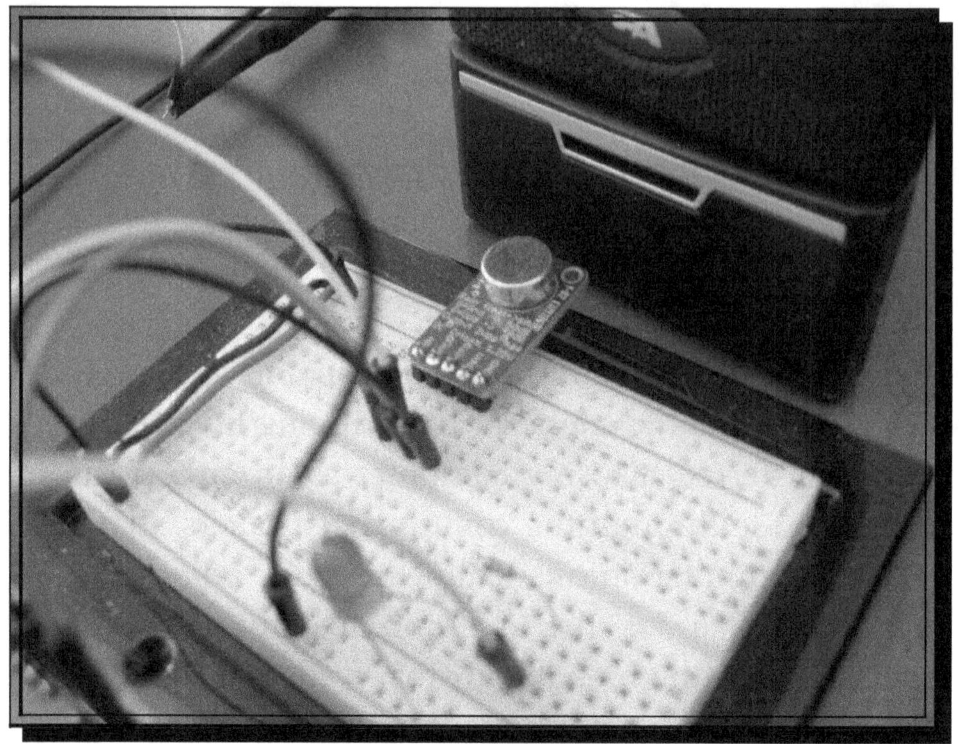

Figure 3-4. Close-up of Microphone

Figure 3-5 shows the schematic diagram for this experiment, and Figure 3-6 is a Fritzing diagram showing the wiring.

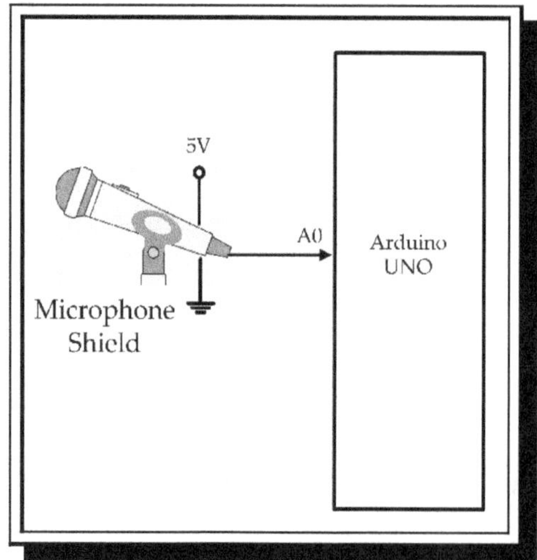

Figure 3-5. Microphone Schematic

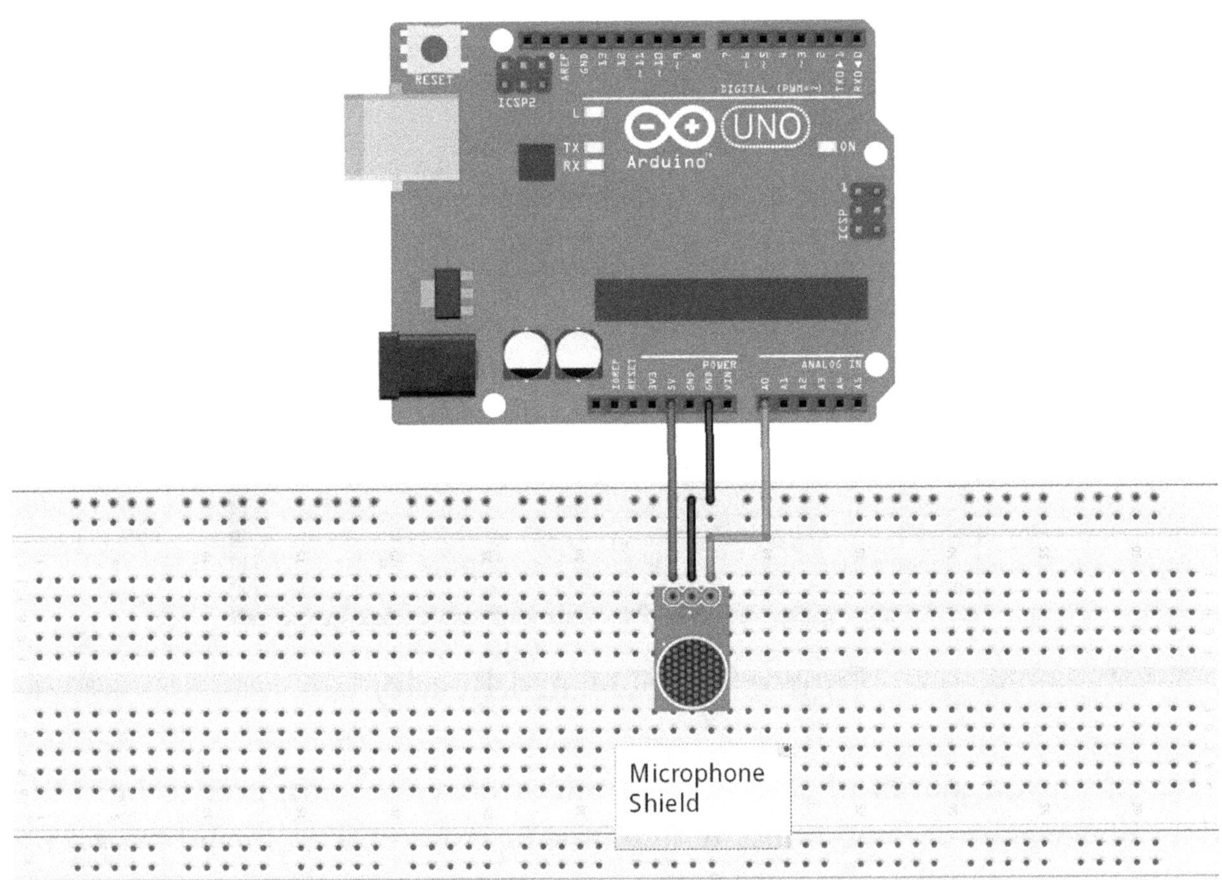

Figure 3-6 Microphone Wiring Diagram

3.2.2 Importing the Data File

Now that we have sampled the recording of the dripping faucet and created a list of numbers (one dimensional array) on the SD card we need to import it into the PC and display it in a way that might reveal any hidden patterns.

Importing the data set is as simple as removing the SD card from the Arduino shield and sticking it in your PC. If your machine doesn't have an SD card slot, you can use an SD card reader with USB connector as shown in Figure 3-7 below.

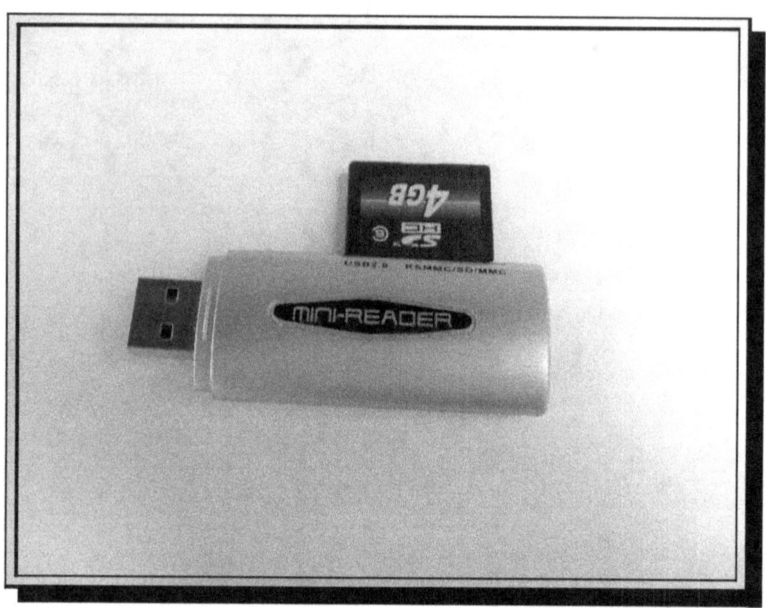

Figure 3-7. SD Card Reader

Then it's just a matter of setting up a folder on your computer to hold the data file. Make sure you know where it is, because you will need to specify the path when you run the BASIC routine. I do all of my file management with Windows File Explorer. That approach helps me to know exactly where everything is. Now we're ready to convert the file to a three-dimensional csv file that the display software can use.

3.2.3 Displaying Our Captured Data

The Arduino sketch for capturing data from analog port A0 is shown in Appendix A and the BASIC routine for file conversion of our captured data from a one-column text file to a three-column csv file is discussed in Appendix D. Figures 3-8 through 3-10 are three different views of the data set derived by sampling the dripping faucet at regular intervals.

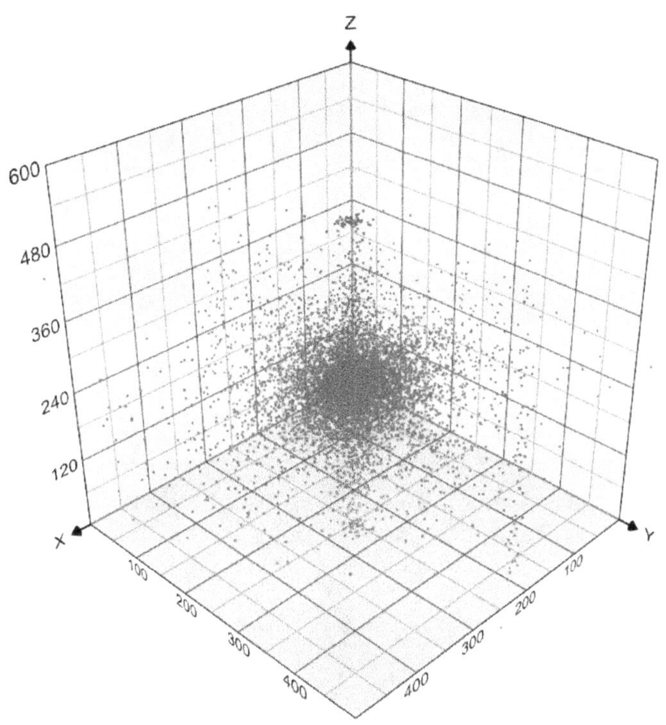

Figure 3-8. Dripping Faucet, View #1

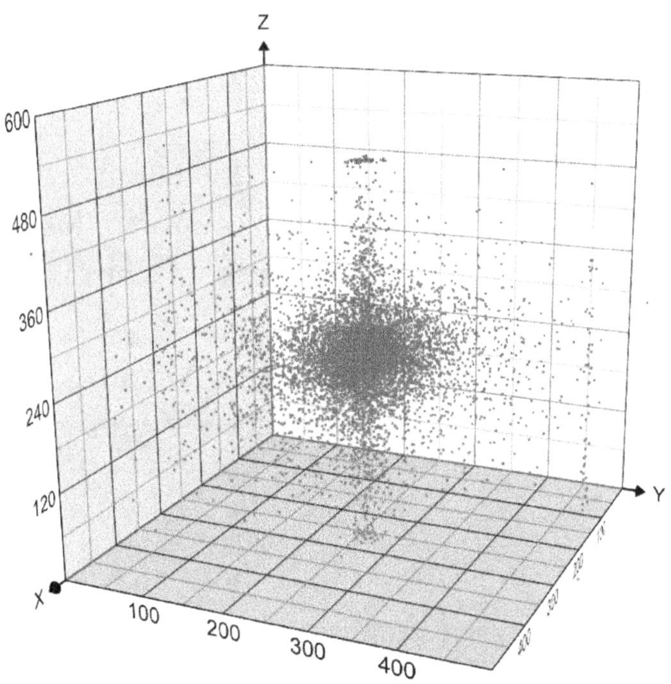

Figure 3-9. Dripping Faucet, View #2

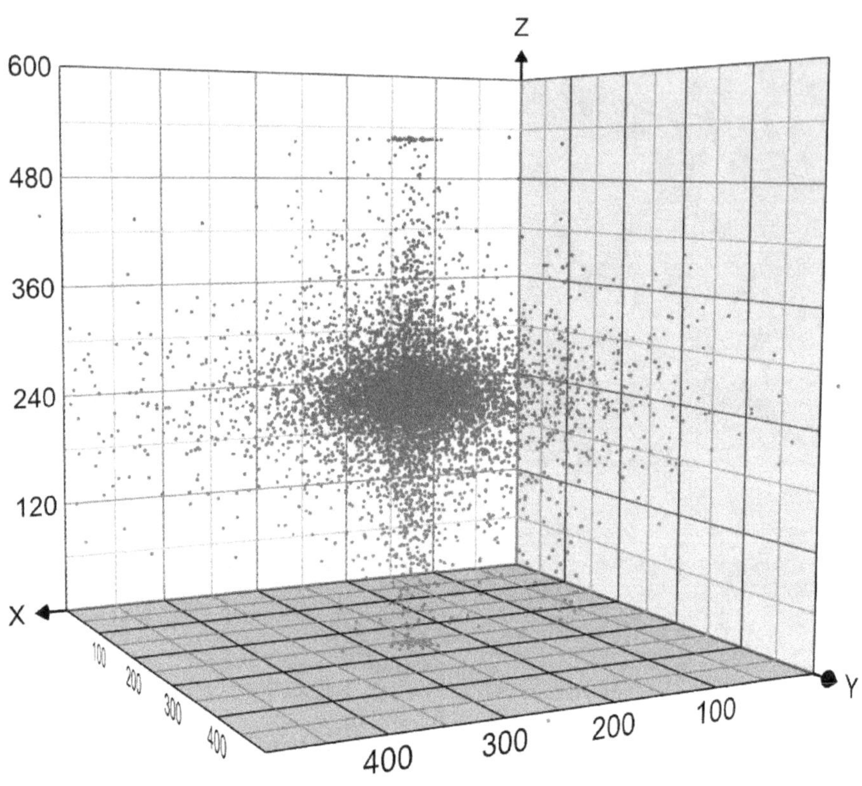

Figure 3-10. Dripping Faucet, View #3

Looking at these figures, you can see that this event, which seemed pretty random when just listening to it, actually has a form. How can we interpret this plot? Keep in mind that these numbers represent a sampling of voltages at regular intervals on the A0 analog port. Those voltages are recorded as numbers from 0 to 1023 by the Arduino A/D converter, and then we present them as a 3-D plot. If there are patterns we are bound to see them!

You may see things that I don't, but here are a few of my initial observations:

1. There is a central clustering of points around coordinates (250,250,250).

2. There is a central "shaft" that extends from (250,250,0) to (250,250,500) with a cluster at each end.
3. There is a "cloud" of points surrounding the central plot.

So how do we interpret what we are seeing in the plot? When I see a "fuzzy ball" I think random as we saw in the plots for white noise and the box fan.

Certainly the central portion appears random, but there is a structure outside of that possibly due to some regularity in the timing of the drops. I would love to hear your thoughts.

In the next section we will see plots based on timing the intervals between drops. Based on the distinct gaps in those plots, the dripping faucet is clearly not completely random.

3.3 A Different Approach: Timing Individual Events

Now, here's a different approach to understanding the same captured audio file. In this case we clean up the signal so we can isolate the time individuals between drops, and then we plot those intervals in 3-D. This may seem like a subtitle difference, but it is a major shift in perspective! After all, when listening to a dripping faucet for patterns what are you listening for? Your brain automatically filters out all the noise and concentrates on the drops themselves. Wow! How amazing!

> If you really want to look for "attractors"
> You need to capture time intervals.

If a natural process consists of a series of events (no matter how much noise there is in the signal) we can find a way to isolate those events and determine the time intervals between them. Then we can create a plot based on those intervals.

Even as I write about it, it seems pretty complicated, but it really isn't.

3.3.1 Capturing Time Intervals

This time, instead of using a microphone, I played the signal out of the speaker earphone jack. That way I could get a much larger signal than the mic could produce. Figure 3-11 is an oscilloscope trace of the captured audio recording. It is pretty noisy, but you can see where the individual drops occur. We need to clean this signal up so we can trigger interrupts based in the individual drops. To trigger the interrupts we need a signal with a nice clean rising edge. The interrupts will determine how much time has passed since the last interrupt (drop) occurred and write that number (in milliseconds) to the SD card.

How can we extract the actual drops from all this noise?

Enter the Schmitt Trigger!

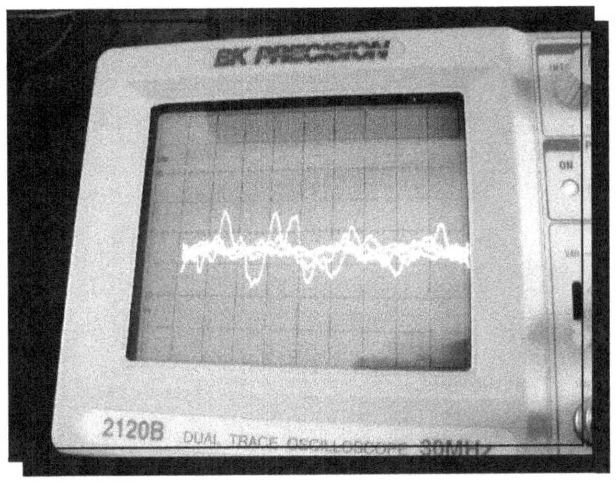

Figure 3-11. Raw Audio Signal

3.3.2 The Schmitt Trigger

The Schmitt Trigger is a simple but amazing circuit. It has hysteresis.

You might be wondering, "What is hysteresis?"
OK, let me give you an example.

We use hysteresis all the time and don't even think about it. Let's say during the winter you set your heater thermostat to 68^0F (my apologies to the rest of the world. We use Fahrenheit over here in the U.S.). So when does the heater actually kick on or turn off?

If the temperature is below 68 degrees we want the heater to come on. Once it gets above 68 degrees we want it to shut off. But, what if the temperature is exactly 68 degrees? Should it turn on or turn off? I think you can see the dilemma. It can't just sit there and chatter.

Without getting into bimetallic strips, mercury switches, and all that stuff, just know that we have to get a little bit above the target temperature for the heater to shut off, and a little bit below the target temperature for it to turn on again. That's called hysteresis!

In the same way, we can clean up a messy signal with a comparator that has some hysteresis built in. If the signal is noisy, but does have some peaks every now and then, we'll use a comparator that will turn on above a certain point, but won't turn off until it reaches a point well below the place where it turned on.

These values are called "trip points." We are using a 5V power supply and the trip points are about one third and two thirds of the supply, so we have trip points of:

1. Upper trip point = 3.3V
2. Lower trip point = 1.6V

The 555 op amp shown in Figure 3-12 is wired as an inverting Schmitt trigger. That means that when the input signal gets above 3.3V the output will go low. Then the input can vary all over the place, but the output won't go high again until the input goes below 1.6V. At that point the reverse is true. The output won't go low again until the input goes above the 3.3V upper trip point.

Figure 3-12 shows a 555 op amp wired as a Schmitt Trigger, and Figure 3-13 shows graphically how it works.

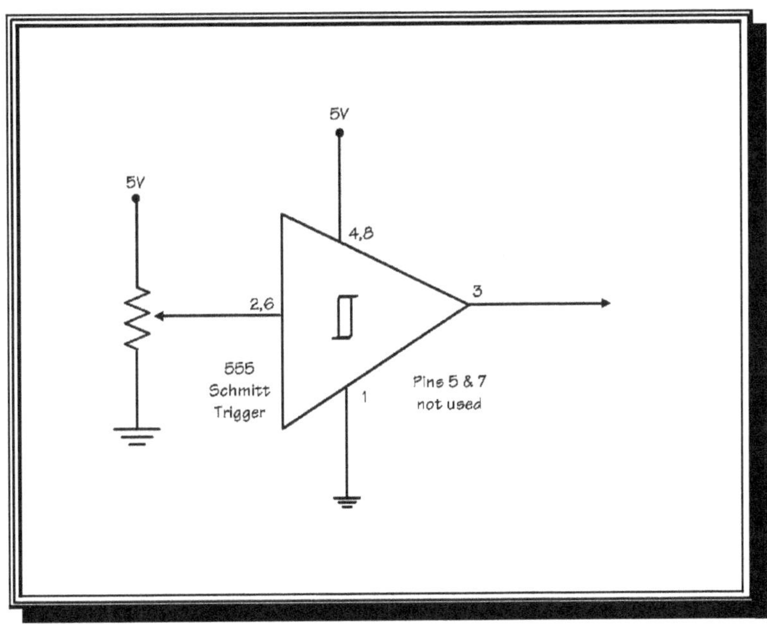

Figure 3-12. The 555 Op Amp Schmitt Trigger

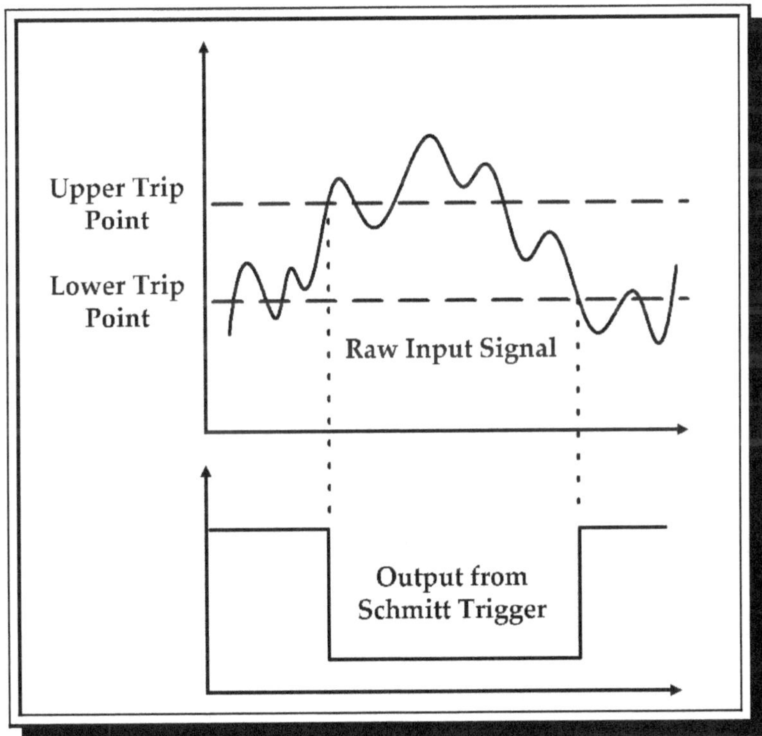

Figure 3-13. Inverting Schmitt Trigger Trip Points

Figure 3-14 shows how we convert a noisy analog signal to a clean digital signal with nice clean rising and falling edges that can be used to trigger interrupts.

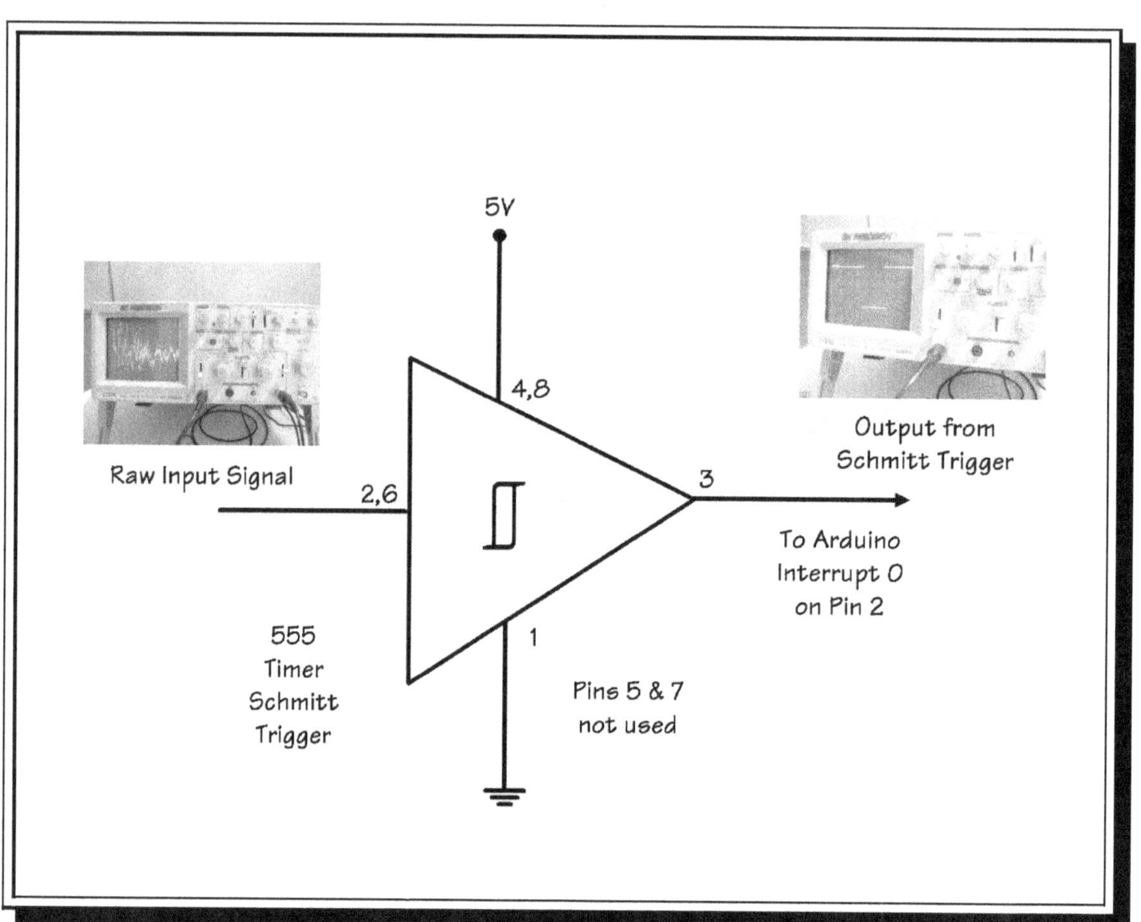

Figure 3-14. Schmitt Trigger Cleans Up Noisy Signal

Now, for this thing to work properly we need the sound of the drops to rise above the upper trip point and then drop below the lower trip point before the next drop. Because we are playing the mp3 file out the earphone jack of the computer speaker we can make its amplitude anything we want (within reason). To center this AC signal on 2.5V, I added a simple voltage divider to offset the signal as shown in Figure 3-15.

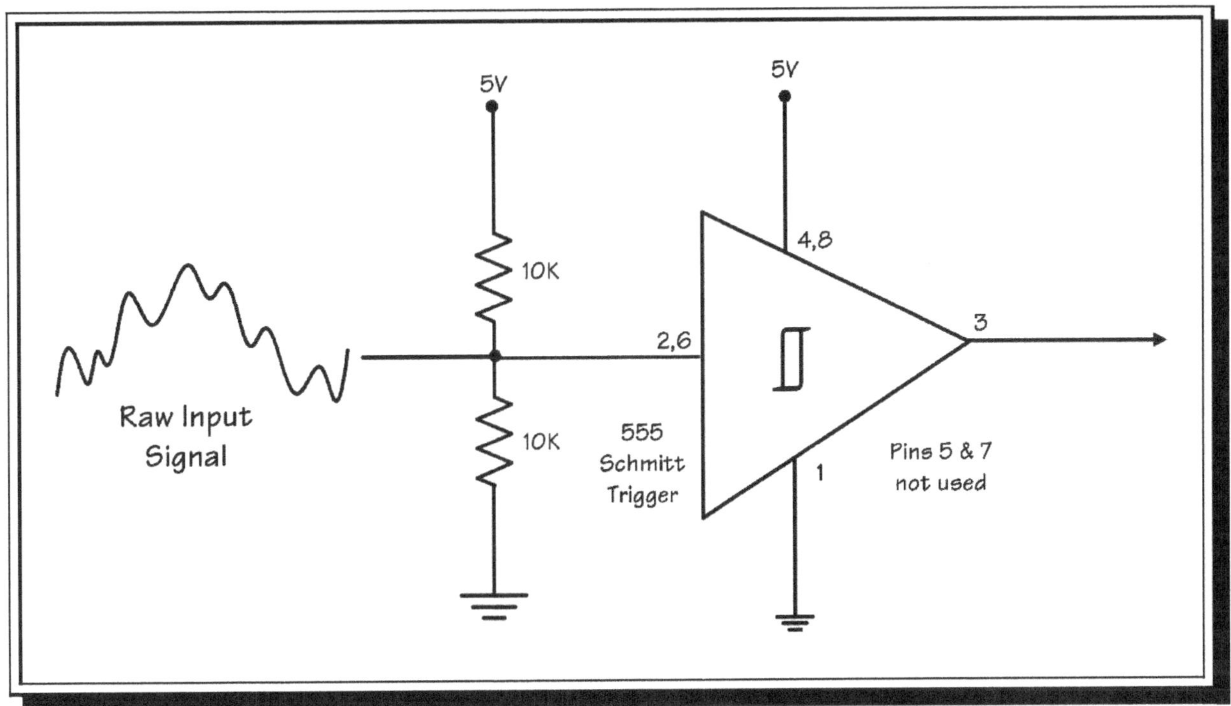

Figure 3-15. Schmitt Trigger Schematic

4.3.3 Interrupts

When you don't want to be constantly checking an input to see if it has changed, and you don't know when a change might occur, what can you do? Let an interrupt take care of it.

It's like when you are expecting an important phone call. You don't want to miss the call, but you don't want to just sit by the phone waiting for it to ring. So you go about your other tasks, keeping an ear out for the phone to ring. You might be busy vacuuming the carpet when the phone rings. What do you do? You stop vacuuming and go answer the phone. When the call is over you can go back to vacuuming.

The Arduino sketch for interrupt-based capture is shown in Appendix B.

Figures 3-16 through 3-20 show five different views of the time intervals between drops. In the first plot the dots look fairly random, but when viewed from various angles a distinct structure is revealed.

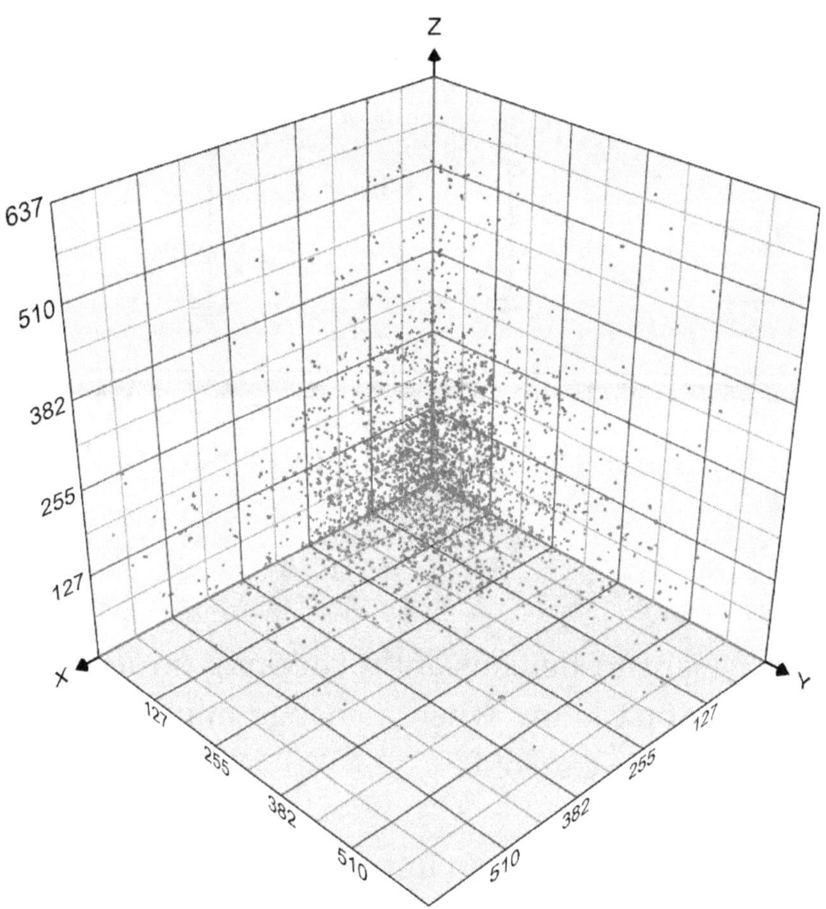

Figure 3-16. Dripping Faucet Time Intervals, View #1

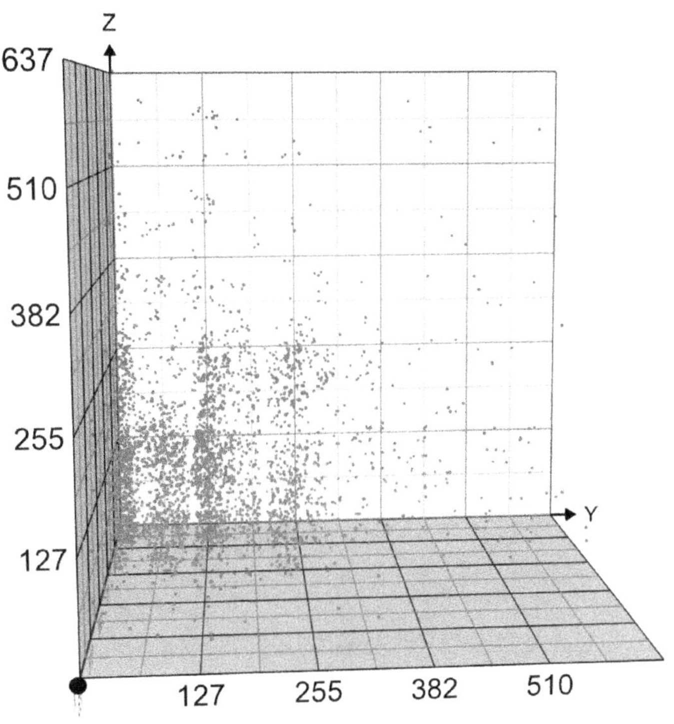

Figure 3-17. Dripping Faucet Time Intervals, View #2

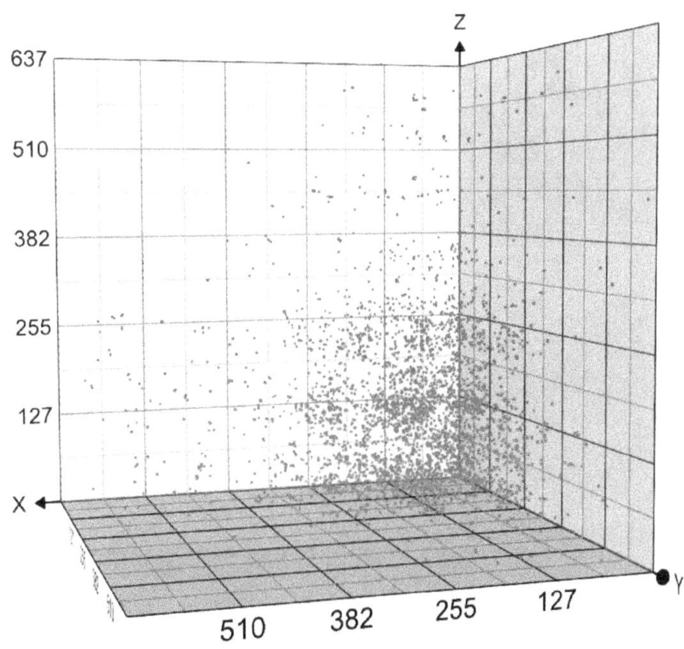

Figure 3-18. Dripping Faucet Time Intervals, View #3

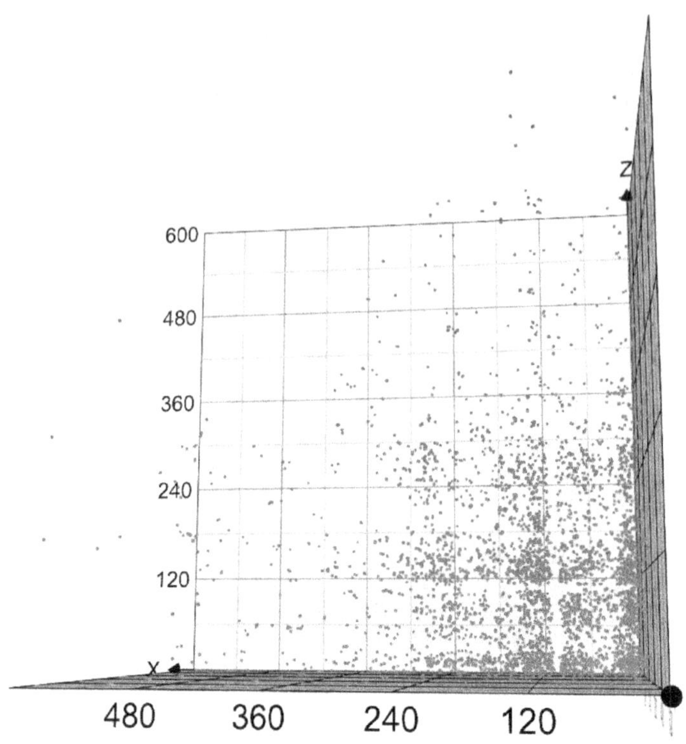

Figure 3-19. Dripping Faucet Time Intervals, X/Z Plane

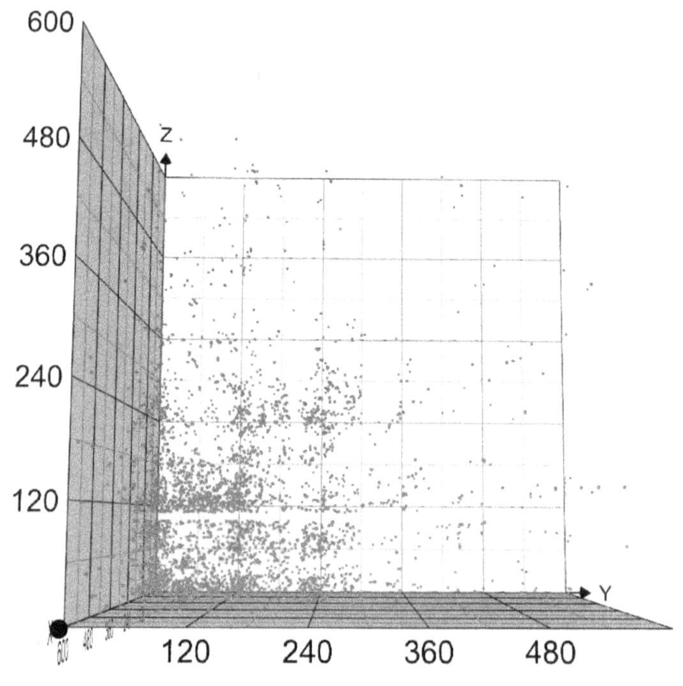

Figure 3-20. Dripping Faucet Time Intervals, Y/Z Plane

3.3.5 Displaying Our Captured Data in 2-D

You would think that a two dimensional plot would contain less information, but displaying the same data set in two dimensions can actually help us understand the 3-D plot. In Figure 3-21 the structure becomes very apparent.

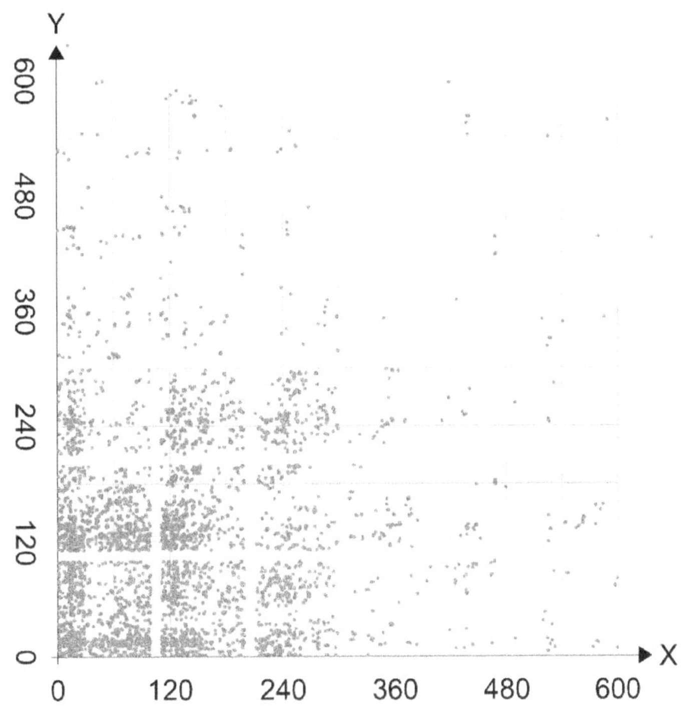

Figure 3-21. Dripping Faucet Time Intervals, 2-D Plot

Chapter 4: Blowing in the Wind: Optical Sensor

On a bright, sunny day the tree branches and leaves cast very clear shadows on my back porch railing. When the wind blows these shadows seem to go crazy! They move around in such an unpredictable way. Is there some pattern to their motion, or is it completely random?

4.1 Measuring the Wind's Effect: Optical Sensor

Figure 4-1 is a simple drawing to illustrate how the movement of blowing tree branches will cast shadows on a photoresistor mounted on the Arduino breadboard.

See how the tree's swaying branches interrupt the sun's rays?

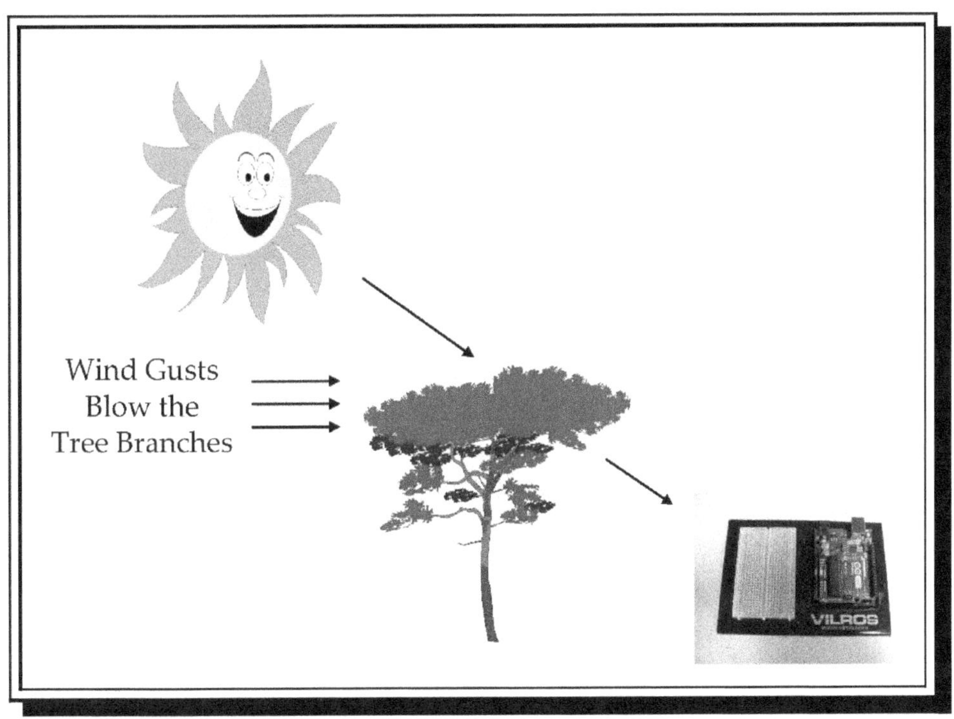

Figure 4-1. Blowing in the Wind

A photoresistor (GM5539) is a special kind of resistor whose value changes with the amount of light that falls on it. In bright light it has very low resistance and in dim light it has higher resistance. To demonstrate this I put an Ohmmeter across a photoresistor and measured its resistance.

In Figure 4-2, you can see that in bright light (the fluorescent lights in my kitchen) its resistance was about 3K Ohms. In Figure 4-3, I blocked the light with my thumb and its resistance went up to about 30K Ohms.

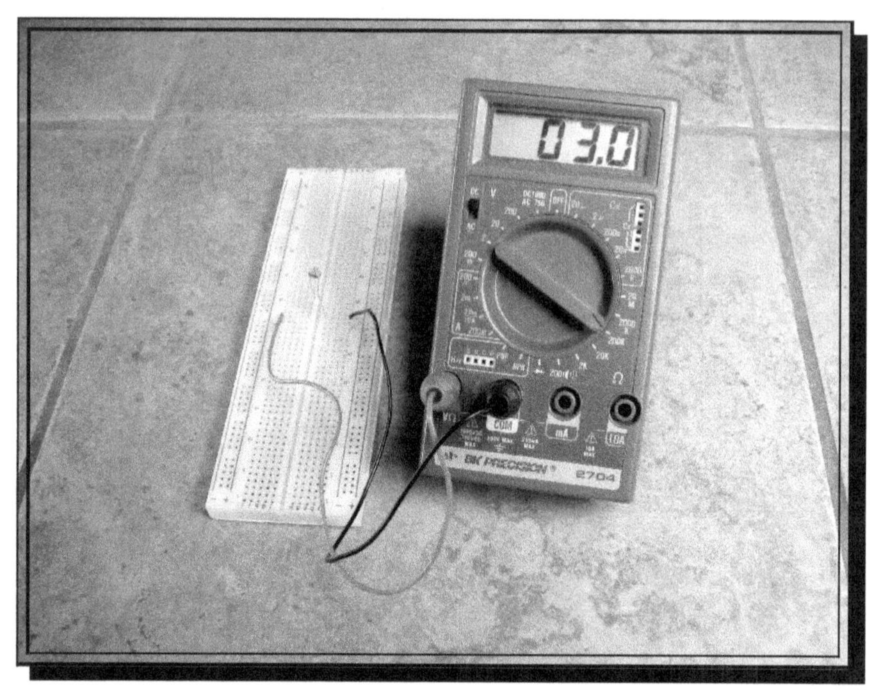

Figure 4-2. Photo Resistor in Bright Light

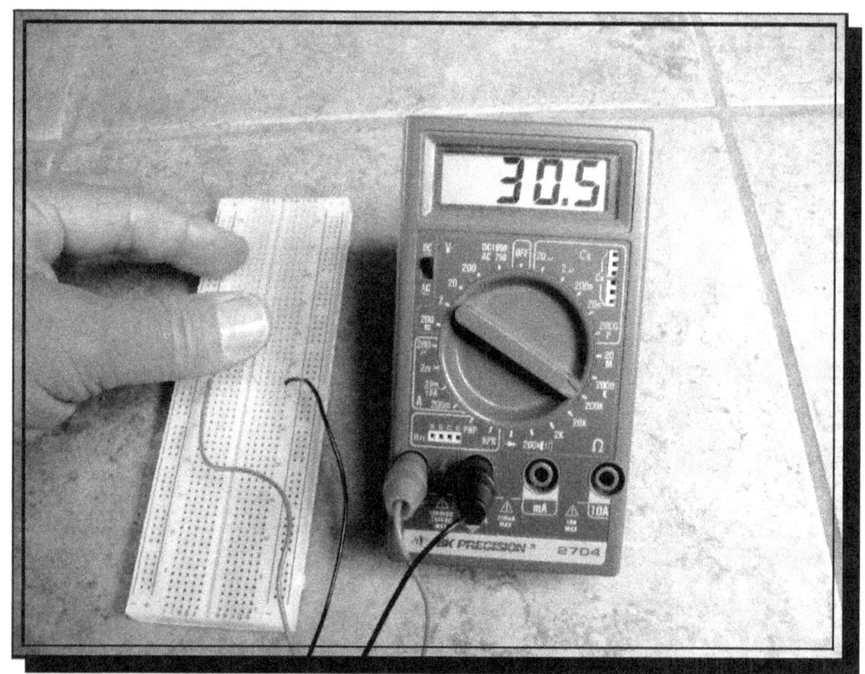

Figure 4-3. Photo Resistor in Dim Light

For this experiment we will use a fixed 10K Ohm resistor and a photoresistor as a voltage divider. This provides a changing analog voltage that we can present to the A0 analog input of the Arduino. How neat is that!

Figure 4-4 shows the schematic for this arrangement, and Figure 4-5 is a Fritzing diagram showing how things are connected. I know it looks pretty simple, but simple is good!

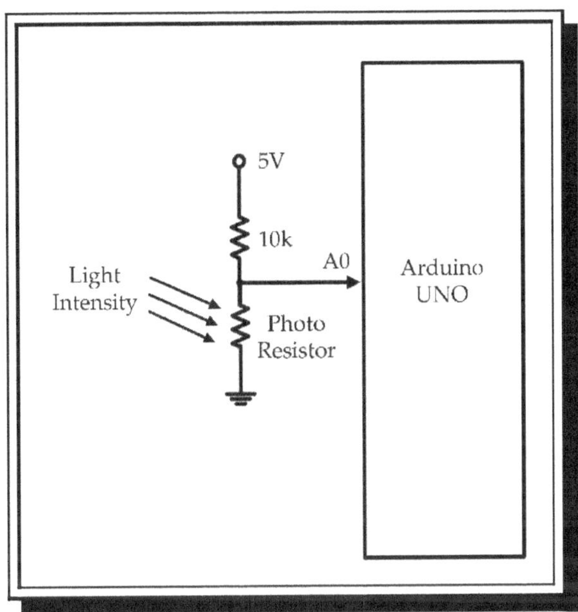

Figure 4-4. Voltage Divider Schematic

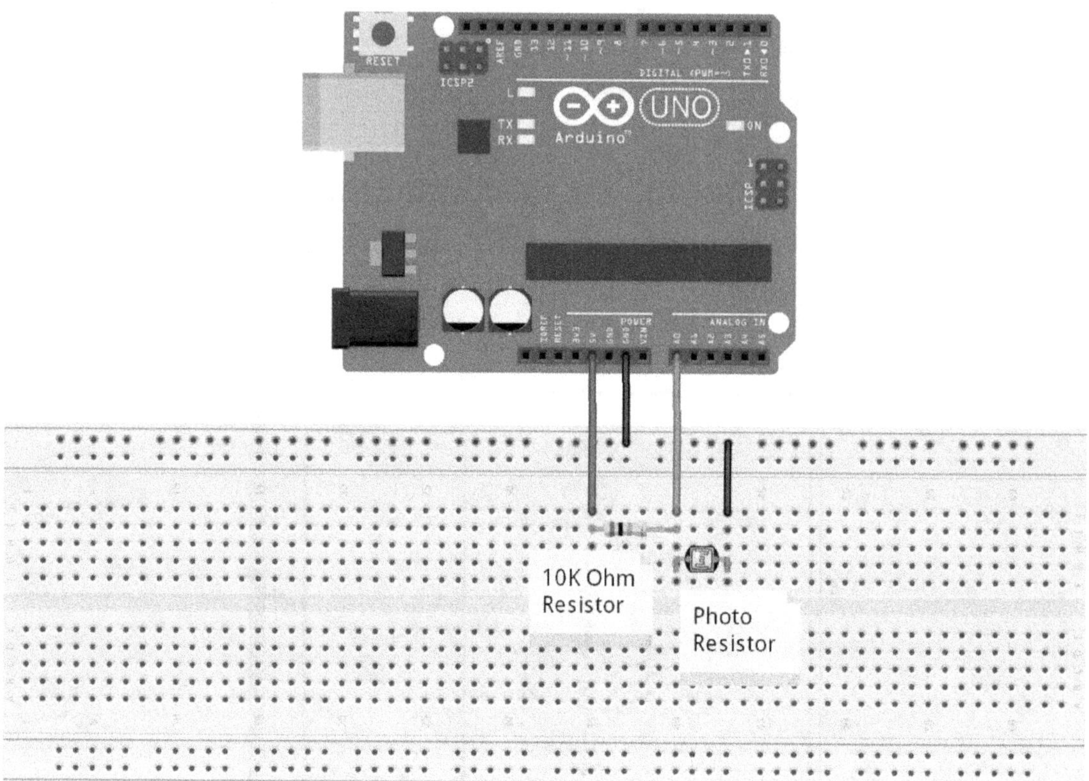

Figure 4-5. Voltage Divider Wiring

4.2 Displaying the Data Set

Figures 4-6 through 4-9 are the same data set viewed from different perspectives. As you can see, this event is pretty complex but certainly not random. What are the forces at work here?

There may be more factors involved, but two things immediately come to mind:

1. Although the wind was coming generally from the west, it was gusting in a complex and unpredictable way.
2. The flexibility and strength of the tree want to return it to its stable "home position."

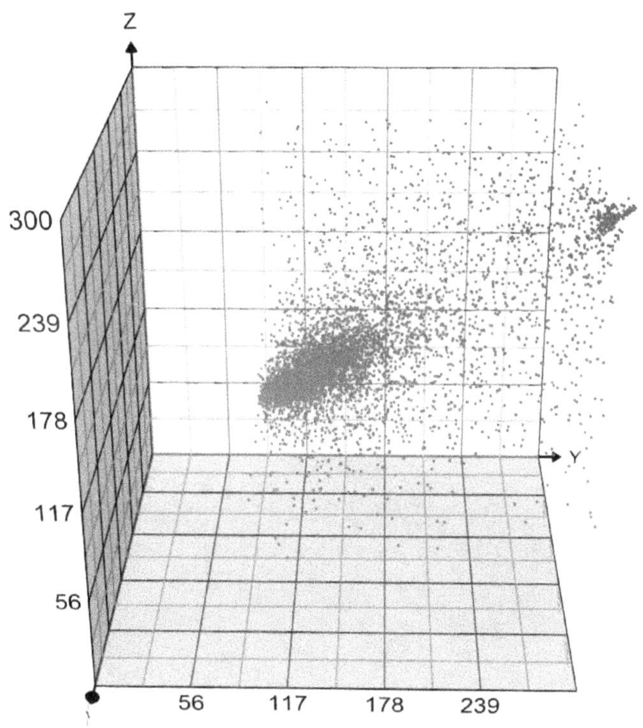

Figure 4-6. Blowing in the Wind, View #1

Figure 4-7. Blowing in the Wind, View #2

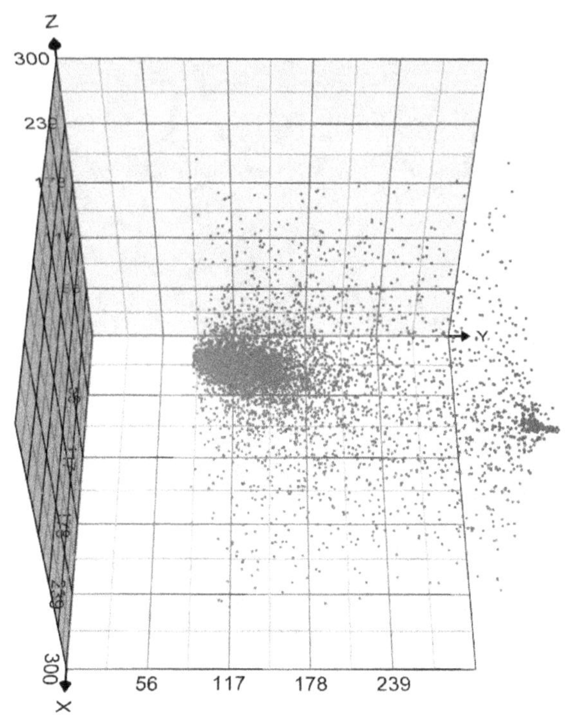

Figure 4.8 Blowing in the Wind, View #3

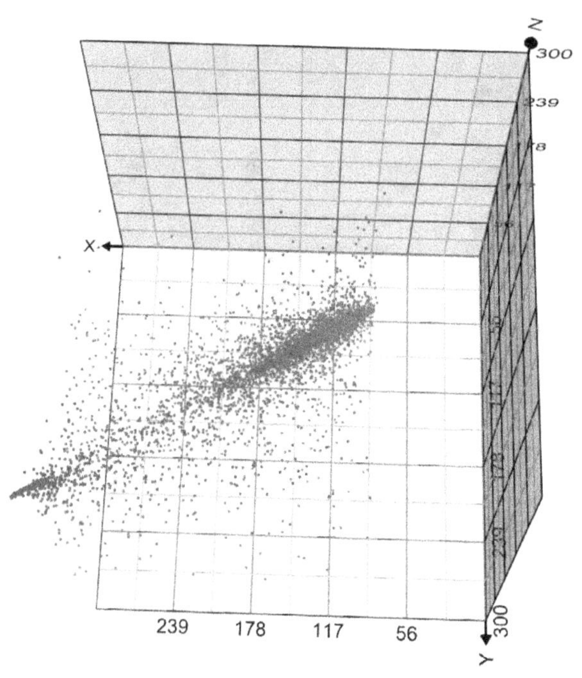

Figure 4-9. Blowing in the Wind, View #4

Looking at the plot, you see a thick and dense central portion with the dots thinning out as you get away from the center.

Keep in mind that the position of the dots is proportional to the light intensity falling on the photo resistor. Each time a sample was taken the brighter the light, the lower the voltage measured. Because the clustering is the greatest at the bottom, I suspect that when the wind stopped blowing the photo resistor was in the light as opposed to being in shadow.

If you want to expand on this experiment you might want to compare the plots you get by placing the photo resistor in the light and in the shade when the wind is stopped. What might you observe?

1. The greatest clustering will be in a different place.
2. The more chaotic the wind, the more spread out the dots will be.
3. If there were no wind or just a few gusts, you would get only one dot or a small cluster.

If you do this experiment yourself, I would love to see what you discovered. Send me an email at rmckeon5@gmail,com

Chapter 5: Blowing in the Wind: Audio Recording

5.1 A Windy Afternoon on My Back Porch

A storm was blowing in from the west and it was really windy. The air had a chill, and the trees were being blown back and forth like crazy. There was excitement in the air! I could sometimes hear the traffic down on White Spar road, and the plastic bag that I had covered my air conditioner with was whipping around. There were all kinds of sounds, but the sound of the wind predominated. I wondered if there was a way to make sense out of the myriad of sounds. So I thought, "Let's just record what's happening out here and see what we come up with!"

5.2 Displaying the Data Set

I'm not too surprised to see that the plot of Figure 5-1 looks like white noise. The wind was blowing very strong and the H2 recorder didn't have a windscreen on it, so we got a lot of noise. We see a cube on the outside because the wind was blowing so strong that the microphone was overdriven and we were getting clipping.

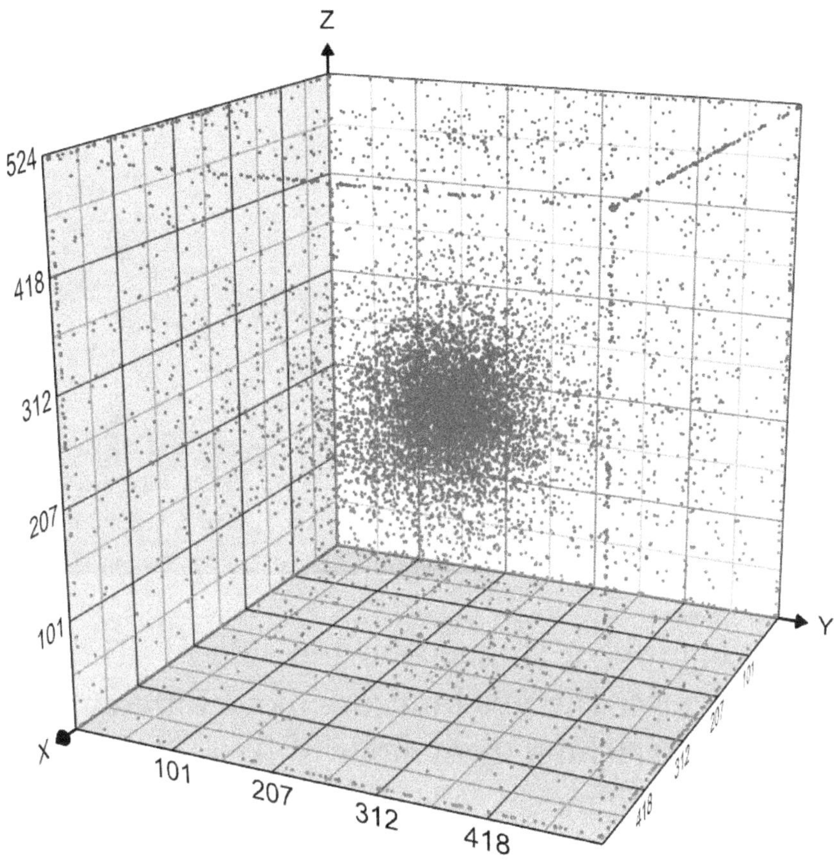

Figure 5-1 Wind Audio Recording

Chapter 6: Blowing in the Wind: 3-Axis Accelerometer

I live in a lovely apartment situated on the side of a hill. This location places me in the treetops. The tree branches move differently up here than they do down below. Watching them move is like watching a lovely dance, and I can almost hear the music. When the wind is strong and gusty, the movement of the branches is very energetic like rock and roll music. When the wind blows more gently it's more like a waltz. But, do they move in a completely random fashion or are there some underlying attractors involved?

The wind can gust in a very complex way, but consider the following:

1. Each tree has a stable place of rest that it will automatically return to when the wind dies down. I think of this home place attractor like the

key signature of a song. There is a strong pull to return. This is based on the size and strength of its branches. Think about the difference between a weeping willow and a ponderosa pine.

2. The stronger the breeze, the further displaced from this "home place" the branches will be.
3. Gusts cause the branches to move in an unpredictable fashion, but are gusts really random? There are many factors affecting them like the overall weather cycle, the local terrain and stuff like that. In fact, I got my best readings on the top of a hill where the canyon below was funneling the wind right up to my location.
4. Would you be surprised to find attractors in a complex system like this?

6.1 Measuring the Wind's Effect

So how do you measure the movement of a tree branch in any meaningful way? At first I thought of all kinds of bizarre and complex ways to do it. I even made up some jigs like a potentiometer with a yardstick handle attached. After thinking about it for a while I realized that not only was that approach cumbersome, it was also restricted to motion in only one axis. So much for the "Rick McKeon Homemade Motion Sensor."

Then I came across a tiny little board containing a 3-axis accelerometer called the GY-521. This little sensor is small and inexpensive, but it is very powerful! So, instead of making my own kluge, I decided to use this excellent little sensor.

After all, we are talking about measuring motion. When measuring stuff, the fewer levels of abstraction the better, and the simpler the better! If I could somehow connect the sensor directly to a tree branch and measure its movement without an elaborate equipment setup that would make the data gathering simpler and more accurate. So let's do that.

Figure 6.1 GY-521 3-Axis Accelerometer

The GY-521 is a tiny board containing a 3-axis accelerometer. As you can see in Figure 6-1, there is a lot of stuff packed on a board about the size of a dime!

The heart of the circuit is the MCU6050 microcontroller. Now, this board is very complex, but we will only connect four wires between it and the Arduino as follows:

1. VCC goes to Arduino 5V
2. GND goes to Arduino GND
3. SCL (Serial Clock Line) goes to Arduino to SCL
4. SDA (Serial Data Line) goes to Arduino SDA

In other words, each of these four pins on the GY-521 goes to the corresponding pin on the Arduino. The SCL and SDA are the serial lines that we will use to communicate with the Arduino. They are part of the I2C serial bus with the Arduino acting as Master and the GY-521 as Slave.

The SD card shield (SD Shield 3.0) that I am using covers the Arduino SCL and SDA pins when it is mounted on the Arduino, so I ran those out with jumper wires to the breadboard. I needed to mount the GY-521 on a tree branch so it could move as the wind blew the branch, so I purchased a couple of RJ45 connectors and used a five-foot Cat 5 cable that I had laying around the house. I soldered the accelerometer directly to one of the connectors, and the other one resides on the breadboard.

The I2C bus has a capacitance limit of 400 pF, which limits the length of cable it can talk through without errors. Category 5 cable has a nominal capacitance of 300pF per 100 meters, so a five foot cable does not present a problem. Figures 6-2 through 6-5 show the arrangement of the Arduino, cable, and accelerometer.

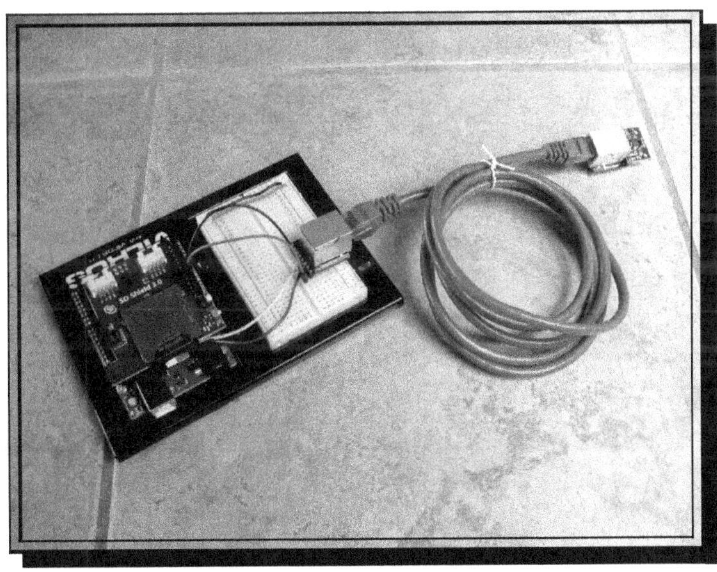

Figure 6-2. Accelerometer Connected to Arduino

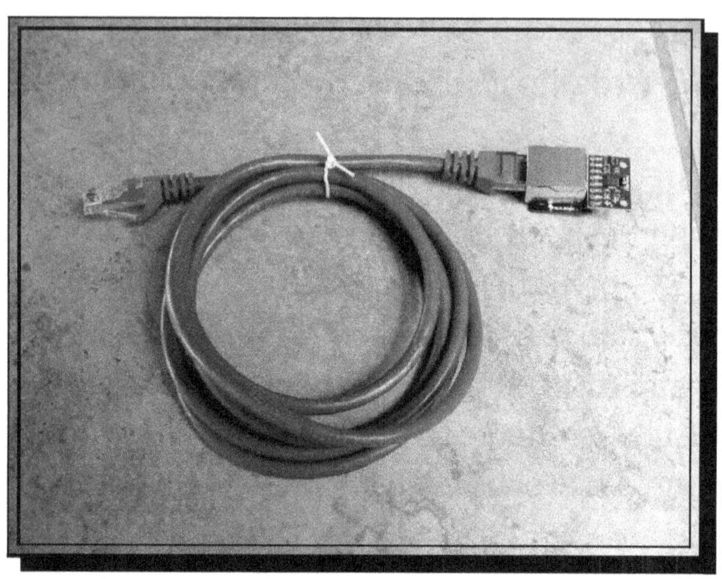

Figure 6-3. Accelerometer and Patch Cable

Figure 6-4. Accelerometer and RJ45 Connector Front

Figure 6-5. Accelerometer and RJ45 Connector Back

Figure 6-6 is a Fritzing diagram showing the wiring from Accelerometer to Arduino.

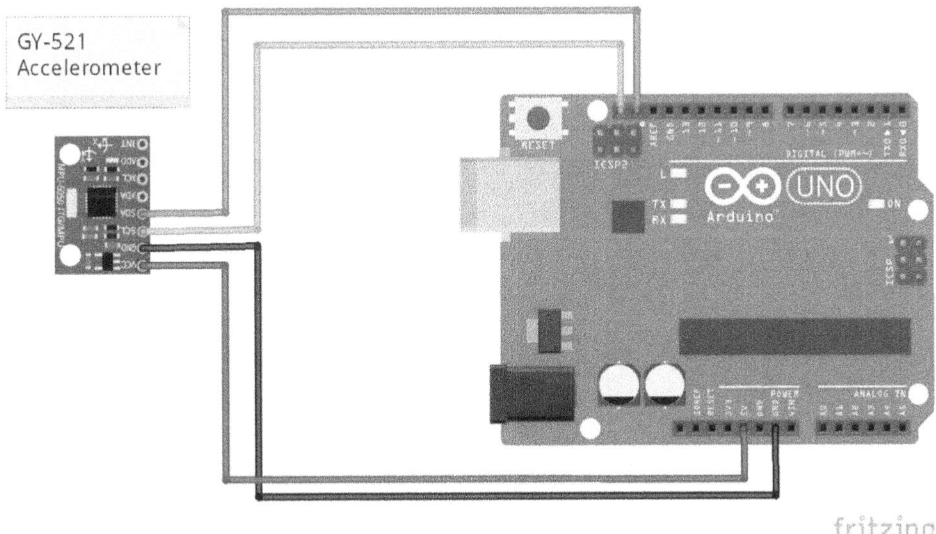

Figure 6-6. Fritzing Wiring Diagram

The GY-521 is capable of a lot more than we are going to ask of it. For this project we are going to simply collect raw data and display it as a 3-D plot. The Arduino sketch for capturing data is described in Appendix C.

6.3 Experimenting at Home

Just to test out the accelerometer I captured four different data sets with 10,000 samples per set. Figures 6-7 through 6-10 are plots derived from just playing around with this amazing sensor. I shook it up and down, back and forth, moved it in a circular motion, and just let it sit on my desk motionless. Now, that's a pretty crude test, and my movements weren't perfect, but you can see in the figures how accurately the plots reflect its motion.

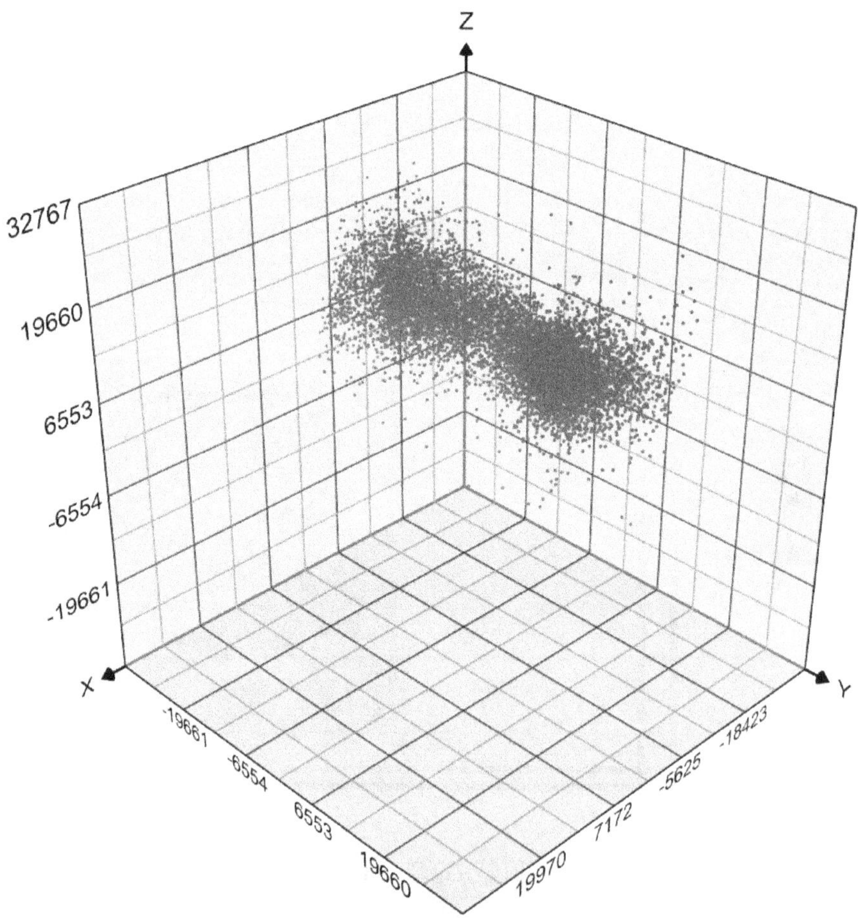

Figure 6-7. Back and Forth Motion

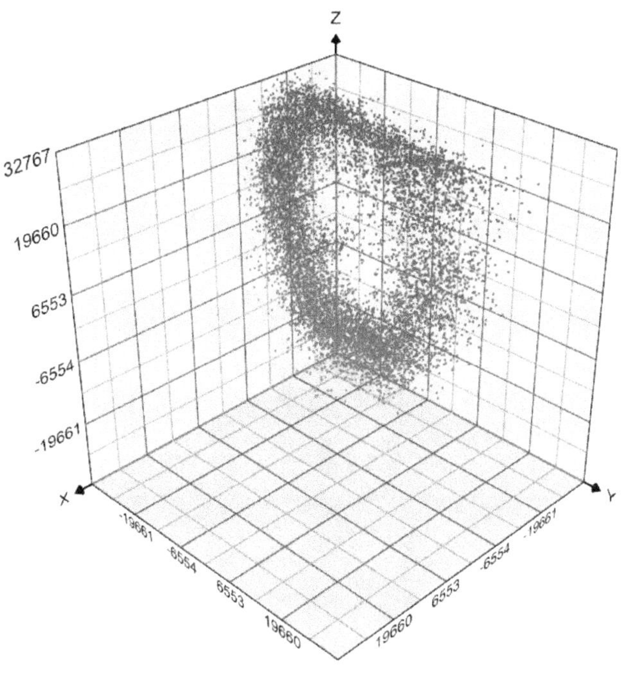

Figure 6-8. Circular Motion

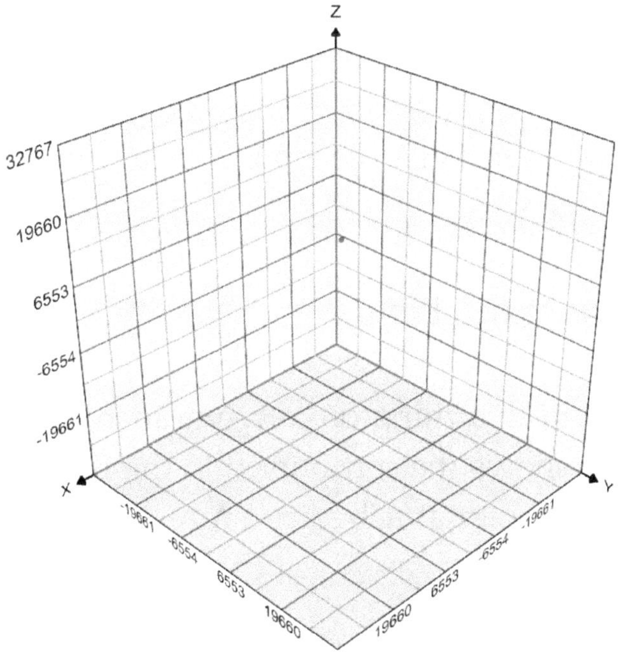

Figure 6-9. No Movement

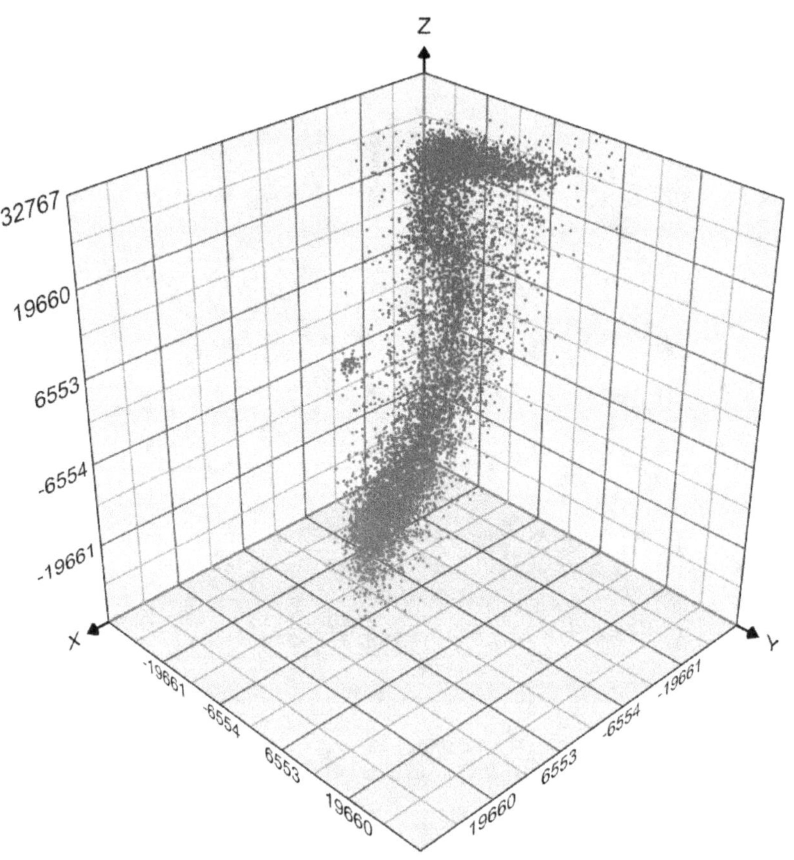

Figure 6-10. Up and Down Motion

OK, now we have a plan. Let's see how we can implement it out in the field.

6.4 Capturing Data in the Field

We are going to mount this thing on a tree branch, so it can, "go along for the ride." Figure 6-11 shows the setup used in the field, and Figure 6-12 is a close up of the accelerometer attached to a branch.

Figure 6-11. Capturing Data in the Field

Figure 6-12 Accelerometer Attached to Branch

6.5 Displaying the Data Sets

Alright, here's the exciting part where we get to view the captured data in three dimensions and try to figure out what's going on.

The plots of Figures 6-13 through 6-18 are from two sample sets (10,000 samples per set) with the accelerometer attached to the same branch in both cases. Figures 6-13 through 6-15 are from the first set, and Figures 6-16 through 6-18 are from the second capturing set. Have a look at them and see what conclusions you can draw. I'll make a few observations after you have had a chance to examine the figures.

On this field trip the wind seemed to operate in two different modes. Most of the time it was fairly moderate but consistent, but then there were times when it would gust pretty strong for short periods. Can you see this behavior reflected in the plots?

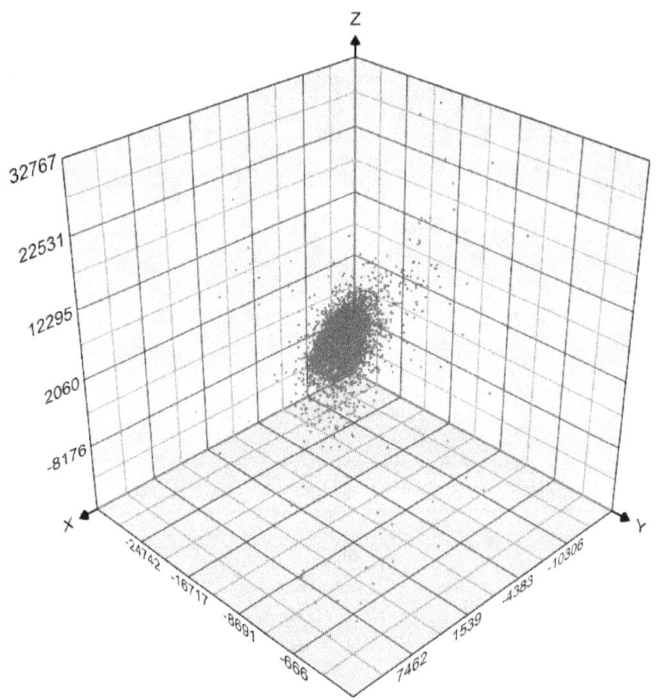

Figure 6-13 Accelerometer Dataset #1, View #1

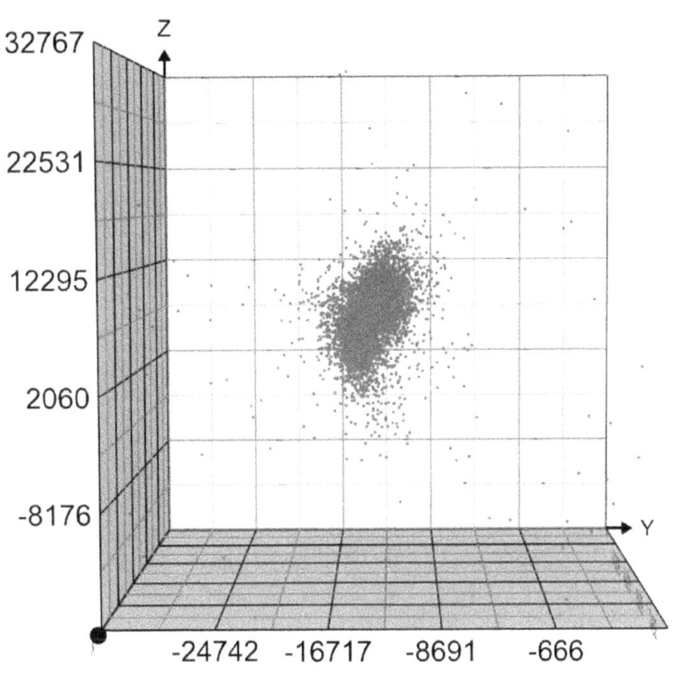

Figure 6-14 Accelerometer Dataset #1, View #2

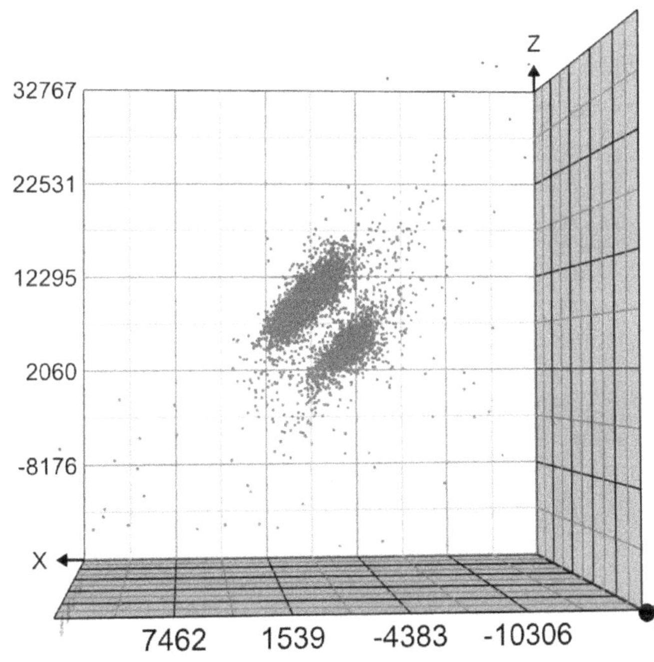

Figure 6-15 Accelerometer Dataset #1, View #3

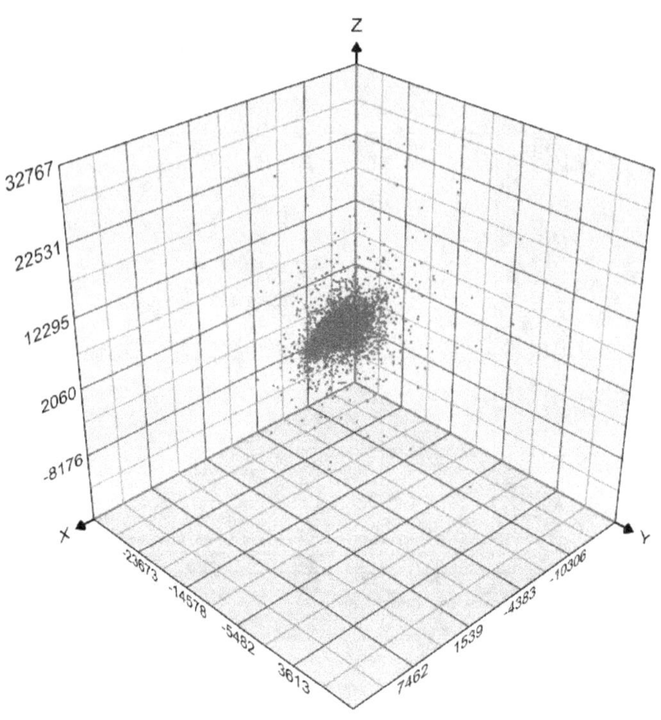

Figure 6-16. Accelerometer Dataset #2, View #1

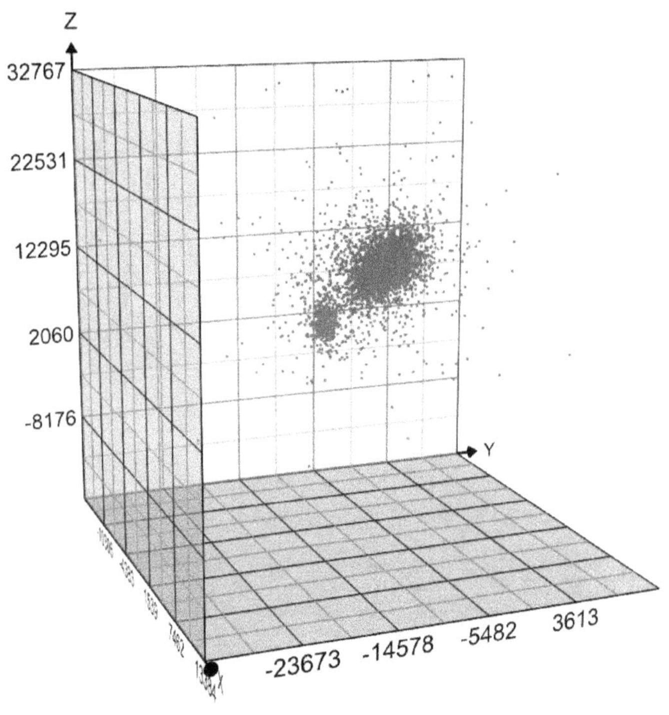

Figure 6-17. Accelerometer Dataset #2, View #2

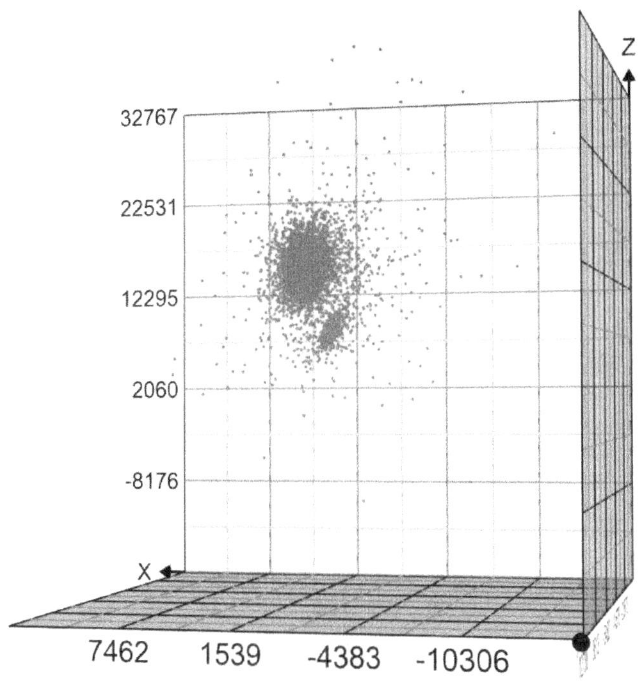

Figure 6-18. Accelerometer Dataset #2, View #3

Something you probably noticed right away is that having the ability to rotate the plots and view them from different angles adds a lot. Otherwise we would have missed the second smaller cluster shown in Figures 6-15, 6-17, and 6-18. These secondary clusters give us a lot more information about the movement of the branch. In each case the cluster looks fairly random like the white noise of Figure 2-28, but they clearly represent the two different modes of the wind. Much of the time the wind was gusting fairly strongly, but even when the wind was calm there was still some motion. Also, these clusters are more elliptical than round (OK, more ellipsoidal than spherical in 3-D talk), which indicates a back and forth attractor instead of free random motion.

Figure 6-15 shows a larger secondary cluster than those in Figures 6-17 and 6-18. Why? During this sampling period the wind was gusting more strongly for a greater percentage of the time.

Bottom line - although we saw two different modes, and an elliptical offset clustering, the movement of the tree branch was pretty random.

Chapter 7: Light on the Water: Reflections

7.1 Beautiful Sparkling Water

Have you ever seen sparkling gems of light reflected from the surface of a lake? What a beautiful and complex sight! I took the picture shown above on a summer afternoon while hiking around Lynx Lake near Prescott, Arizona. I knew I had to come back and capture the reflections.

Are these sparkling diamonds just a wonderful random display, or are there deep underlying patterns at work? If the wind and water just produced steady waves there would be an obvious pattern, but these bouncing wavelets together with the angle of the sun and the gusting of the wind seem to create an unpredictable display.

7.2 Taking Measurements

How can we capture information from this lovely scene? In this case we are talking about reflected light and the reoccurrence of bright sparkling flashes. When we look at the lake it appears we are seeing a multitude of flashes every second in a random fashion. I needed a way to capture and analyze the scene.

So I bought a cheap plastic "kids" telescope on eBay for $14.00.

Can you believe for $14.00 it was brand new and included the tripod, two eyepieces, and free shipping?
Actually, the tripod broke first time out, but I was still able to use it.

7.3 The Sensor

I fitted one of the eyepiece barrels with a 3DU5C phototransistor that will allow us to measure the light variations. The phototransistor has a very low resistance when light shines on it, and a very high resistance when the light is dim. On the Arduino breadboard I built a voltage divider using the phototransistor together with a 1K-Ohm fixed resistor to feed analog port A0 of the Arduino. This phototransistor is much more sensitive than the photoresistor we used in Chapter 4.

The phototransistor has a little tab next to one of the legs that marks the emitter. That leg goes to the lower voltage potential. Just to make it convenient out in the field, I used a red wire for the collector (goes to +5V) and a yellow wire on the emitter (tied to resistor and Arduino A0). As shown in Figure 7-1, I placed the phototransistor above the fixed resistor. Therefore, when the light is brighter, a higher voltage is presented to the Arduino.

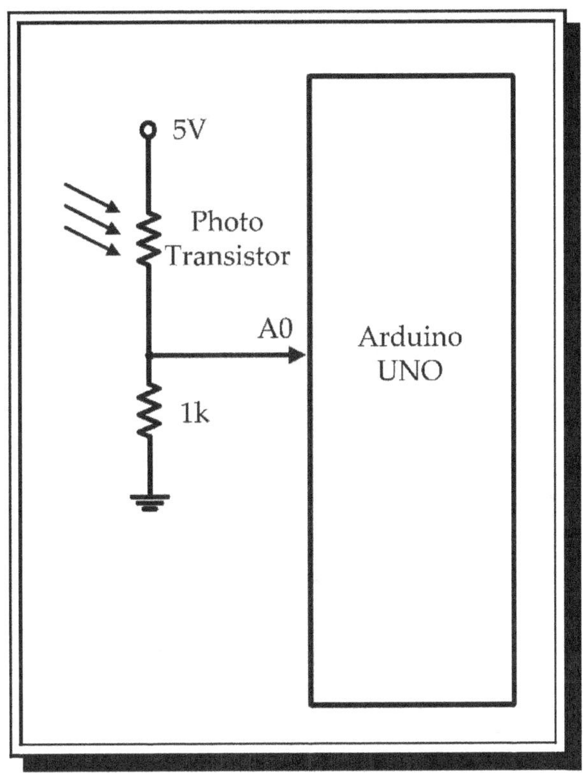

Figure 7-1. Phototransistor - Fixed Resistor Voltage Divider

The cap from the eyepiece canister (kind of like the old 35mm film canisters, if you remember those) fits nicely on the eyepiece barrel, so a little super glue later I had a phototransistor eyepiece! I'm sure the optics in such an inexpensive telescope aren't very good, but I was just interested in capturing the fluctuations in brightness over time. In fact, I didn't even use the optics. I just used the telescope tube as a way to block out stray light, and as a convenient way to hold the modified eyepiece. At fourteen bucks I'm not worried about scrapping it out for parts.

Figure 7-2 shows the eyepiece, its canister, and the phototransistor. Figures 7-3 through 7-8 show how I was able to substitute the phototransistor for the eyepiece lens. This may not be a big budget, precision scientific instrument, but it works. Because I used 22 Gauge solid wire, the eyepiece can plug directly into the Arduino breadboard.

Figure 7-2. Eyepiece, Canister, and Phototransistor

Figure 7-3. Eyepiece Removed from Barrel

Figure 7-4. Cap Fits Nicely on Eyepiece Barrel

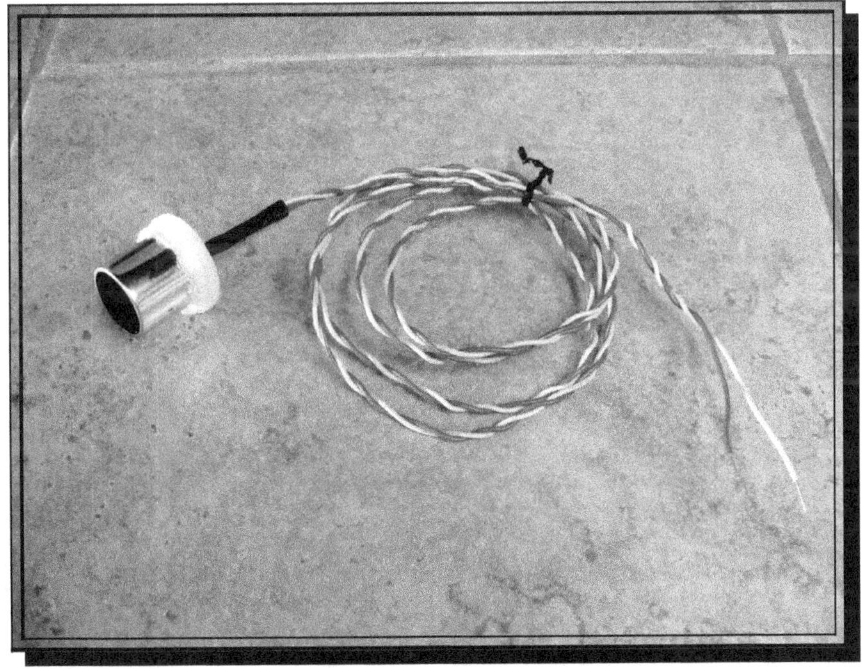

Figure 7-5. The Finished Product

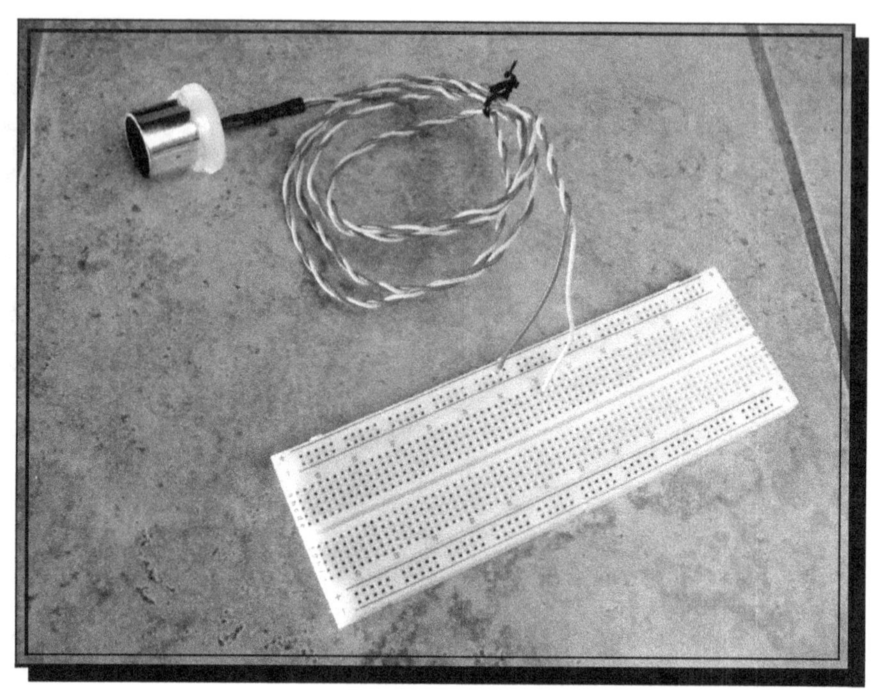

Figure 7-6. Phototransistor Eyepiece and Breadboard

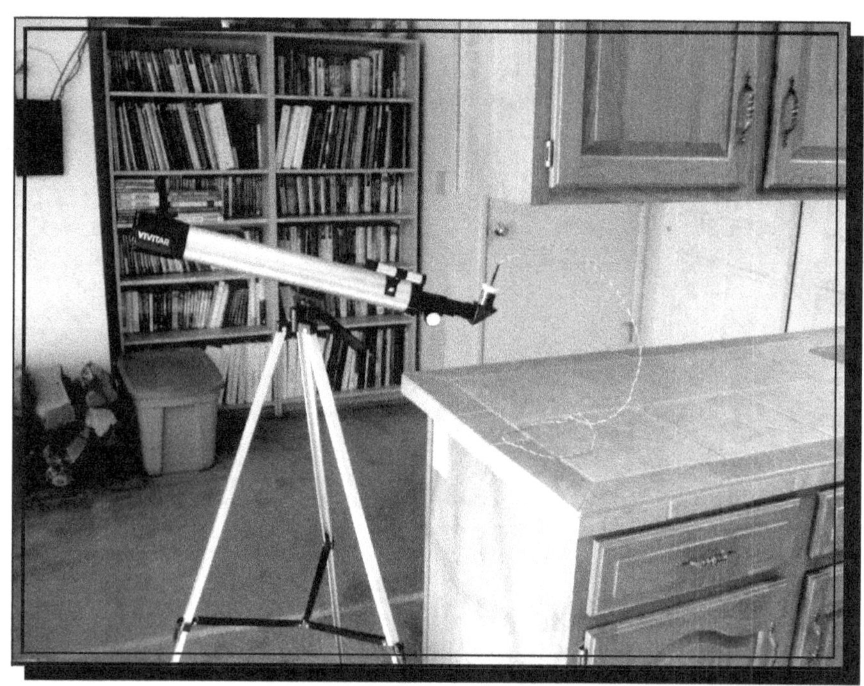

Figure 7-7. Telescope with Phototransistor Eyepiece

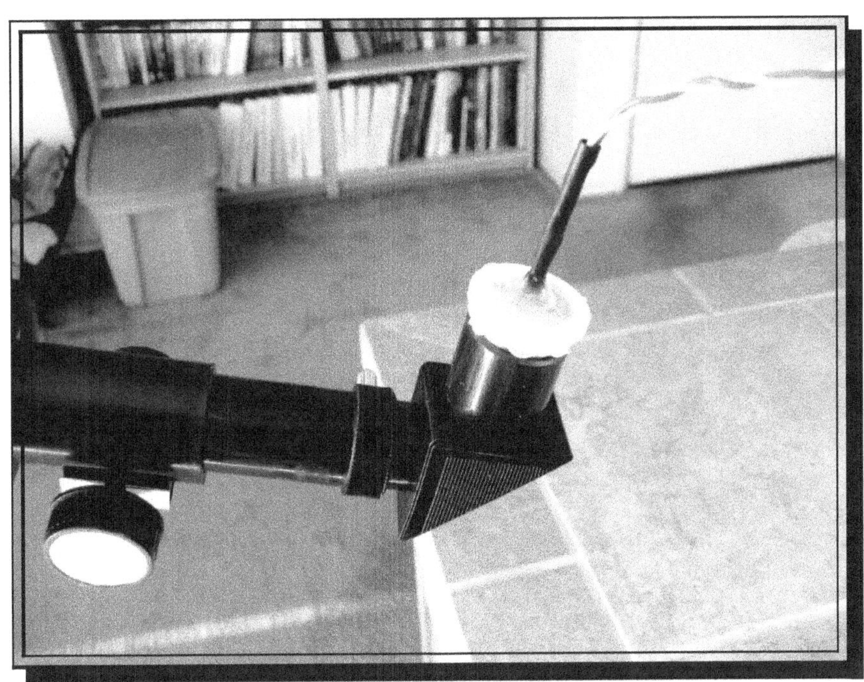

Figure 7-8. Close-up of Eyepiece

Figure 7-9 shows the wiring arrangement used in this experiment.

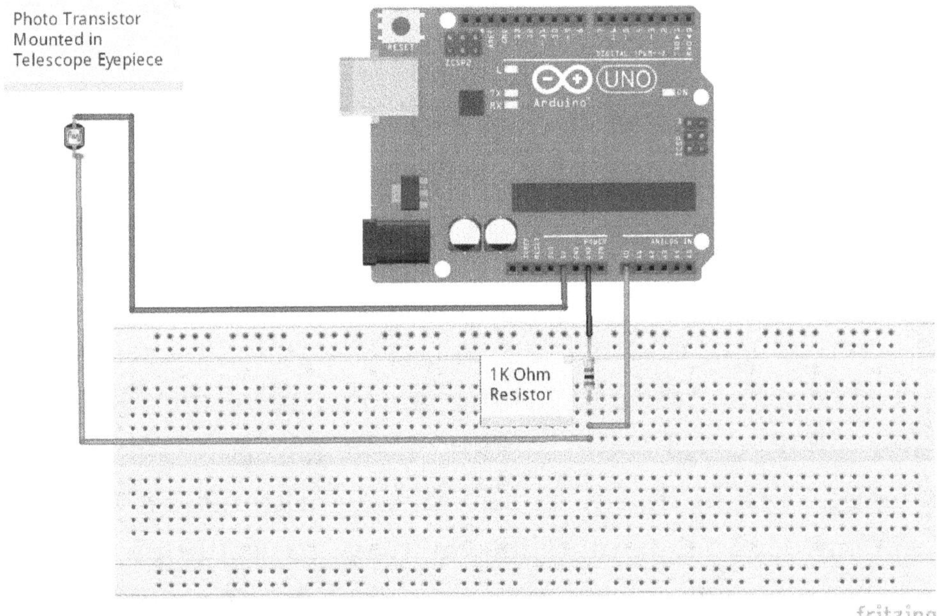

Figure 7-9. The Photoresistor Arrangement

Figure 7-10 shows the optical arrangement with the phototransistor replacing the eyepiece. (OK, so I've removed the objective lens, but this diagram helps make sense of the optical arrangement).

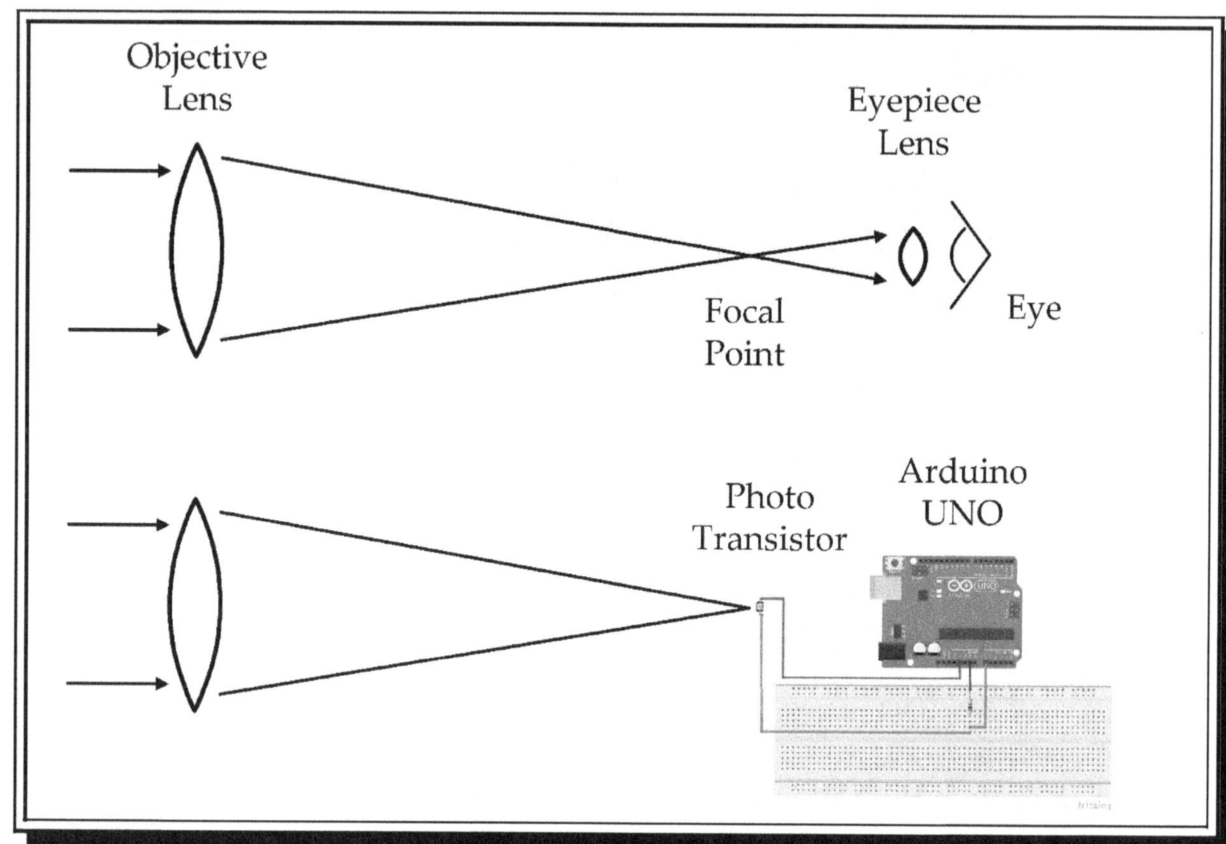

Figure 7-10. Optical Arrangement

Just to make sure that I could capture data under varying light conditions I tested the arrangement on my back porch before taking it out in the field. Figure 7-11 shows the test bed arrangement. I have an adjustable neutral density filter (NDF) that I could mount on the telescope tube if the ambient light was just so bright that it turned the phototransistor ON and kept it turned ON hard. That would be a way to calibrate or "tune" the phototransistor to varying light conditions, but it was not necessary.

Figure 7-11. Testing Light Levels on My Back Porch

Figure 7-12 shows the setup for data capture out at Lynx Lake in Prescott, Arizona. Because we are out in the field capturing with the Arduino I carry a few extra SD cards and capture several datasets.

Figure 7-12. Capturing Reflections from Lynx Lake

One thing I noticed while out in the field capturing data is that the SD card you are writing to can make a big difference in how long it takes to capture 10,000 samples. These days I only carry Class 10 SD cards. Of course, tomorrow they will be ancient history!

7.4 Displaying the Data Sets

With the reflections dancing all over the place could we possibly discover any patterns? I certainly couldn't detect any by just looking at the scene. It was a beautiful display, but very complex.

Once you see the plots I think you will have to agree that this reflected light phenomenon may be complex, but it certainly isn't random. Like all things in nature there are attractors involved. Waves can exhibit a fairly predictable pattern, but what we are seeing here is complexity on top of the waves.

It was a warm day and I had to hike halfway around the like to get in the right position to see the reflections properly (not that I don't like hiking), so I captured three data sets just to make sure that I came home with some good data.

Figures 7-13 through 7-15 were generated from dataset number one. The first plot doesn't reveal very much, but as we view it from different angles we start to understand it better.

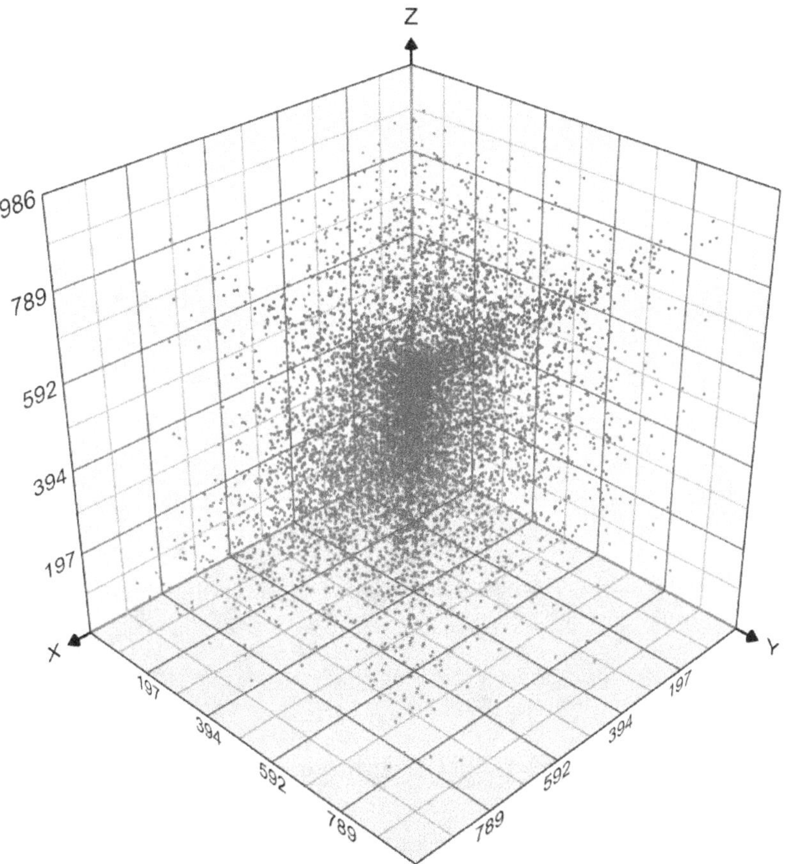

Figure 7-13. Reflections Dataset #1, View #1

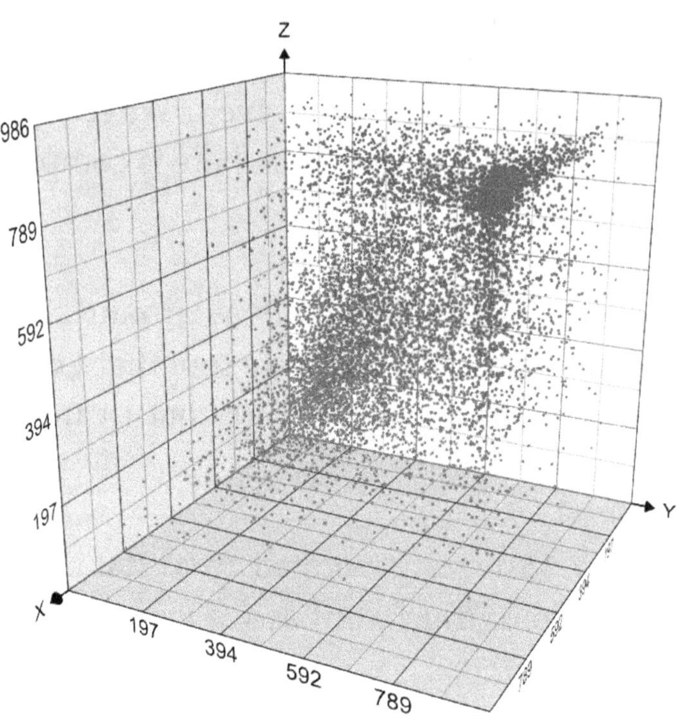

Figure 7-14. Reflections Data Set #1, View #2

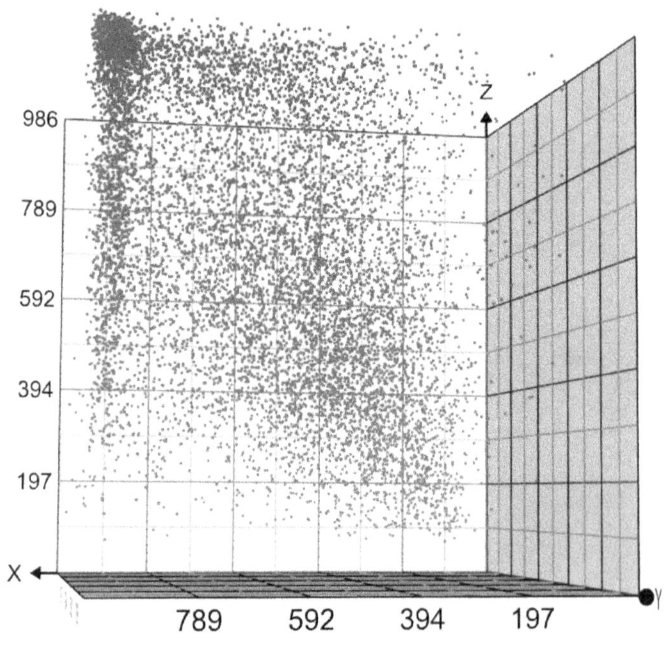

Figure 7-15. Reflections Dataset #1, View #3

Figures 7-16 through 7-18 were generated from dataset number two. There is a strong concentration in the lower numbers, which indicates that the wind was calmer throughout this capture cycle.

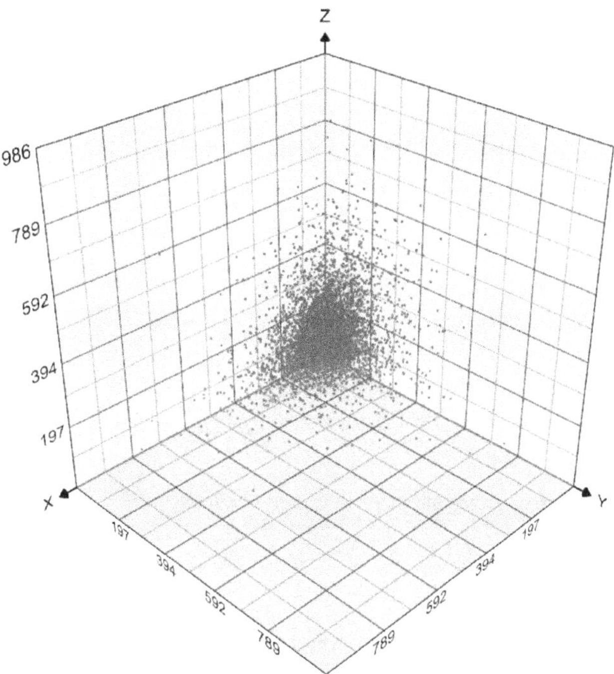

Figure 7-16. Reflections Data Set #2, View #1

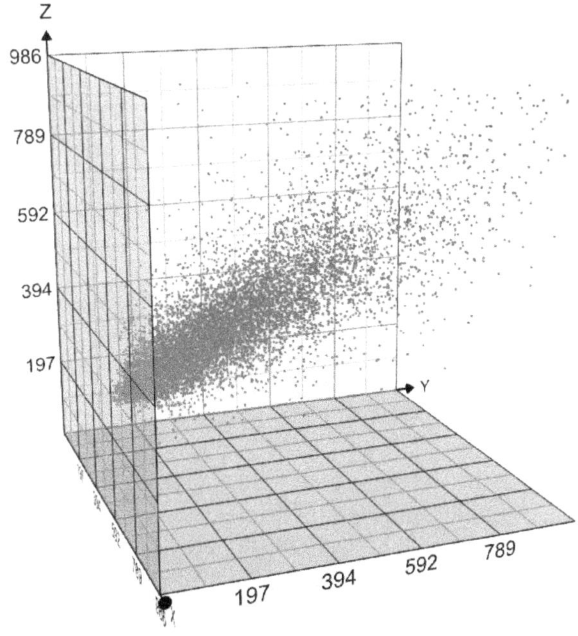

Figure 7-17. Reflections Data Set #2, View #2

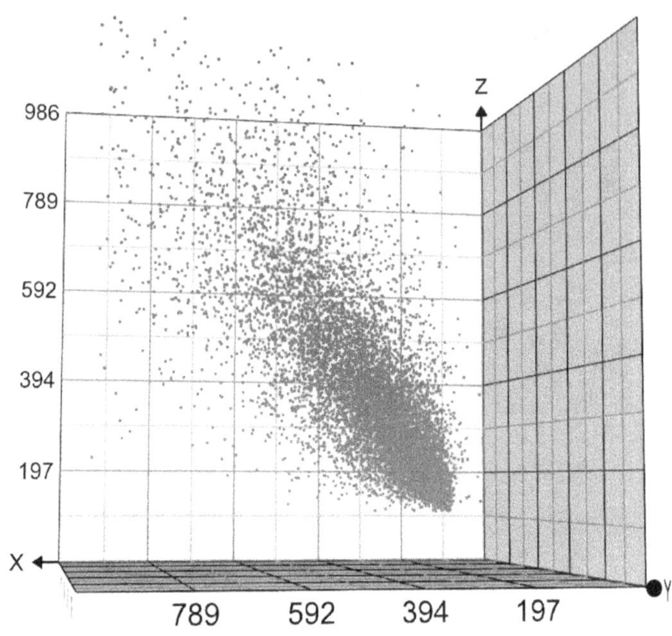

Figure 7-18. Reflections Data Set #2, View #3

Figures 7-19 through 7-21 were generated from the third dataset. During this capture cycle there was a period where the wind died down and the readings were fairly low. Why would the readings be low? The brightest flashes appear when the sun is reflected directly onto the phototransistor. When the wind dies down we are just catching ambient light reflected off the lake's surface. In the plots you can see two distinct clustering of dots - one when the wind was blowing strong and one when it was calm.

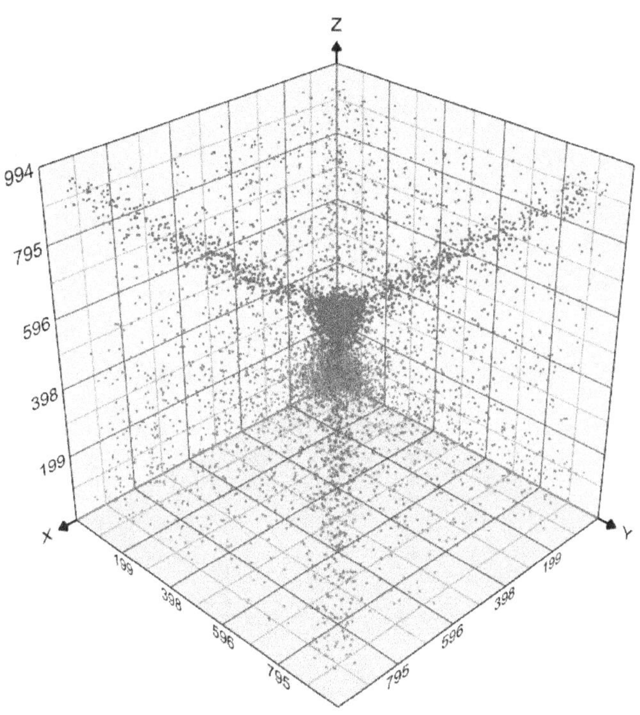

Figure 7-19. Reflections Data Set #3, View #1

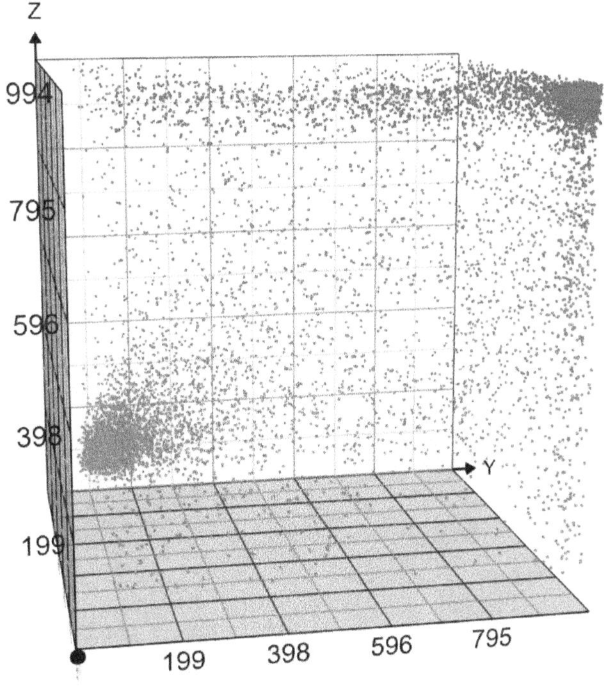

Figure 7-20. Reflections Data Set #3, View #2

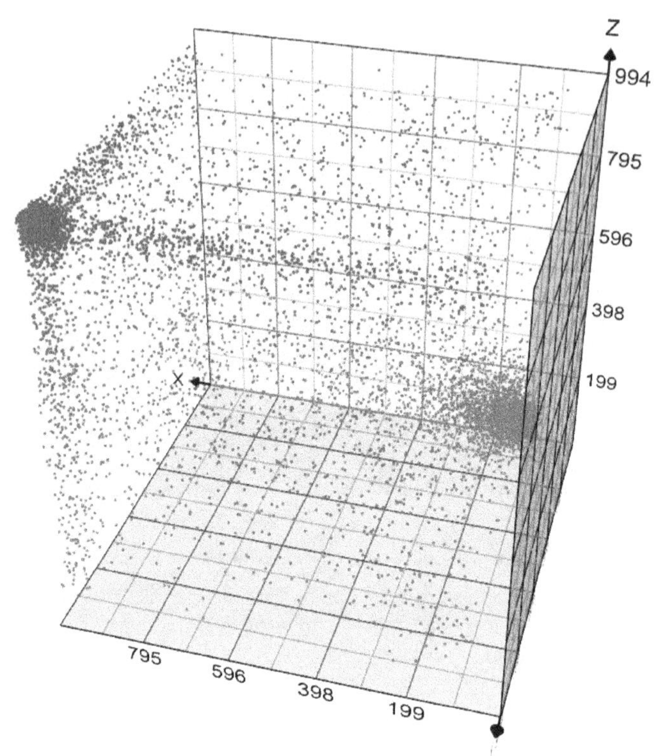

Figure 7-21. Reflections Data Set #3, View #3

Chapter 8: A Babbling Brook

8.1 A Lovely but Complex Sound!

If you sit quietly near a rushing stream you will hear an amazing symphony. If you really listen you will hear higher and lower pitched sounds. Near a little waterfall the drops of water splash on rocks and splash back on the water's surface. You will hear larger and smaller drops make their characteristic sounds. All these things make for a lovely but complex sound. Sometimes I think I hear a reoccurring pattern, but usually it sounds completely random. Could there be hidden patterns in there somewhere? The overall flow rate of the stream is consistent and the rocks remain in their respective positions. Maybe these influences could contribute to some recurring patterns.

8.2 Understanding the Influencing Factors

How can a dynamic system go from one "mode" to another? In a flowing stream you will notice that different parts seem to behave differently. In some places it appears to flow smoothly and in other places it becomes turbulent. When the flow rate gets to a certain point the water tends to become turbulent. Also, behind a large rock you will often find turbulence. The influencing factors may be very complex, but that doesn't mean that we can't understand the system a little bit.

8.3 Capturing Sound

I used a Zoom H2 voice recorder to capture the sound of the stream. Of course the Arduino together with a microphone could be used to capture the sound directly, but this approach seems easier to me.

The circuit and Arduino sketch are the same ones we used in Chapter 5.

8.4 Displaying the Data Set

Figures 8-1 through 8-3 show the plot from three different angles. Of course there is a center frequency, but the plots look very random, almost like white noise. I thought I was hearing some repeating patterns, but I was probably reading something into it. Curious observation!

So, here's an interesting question:
Can we hear patterns where there are none?

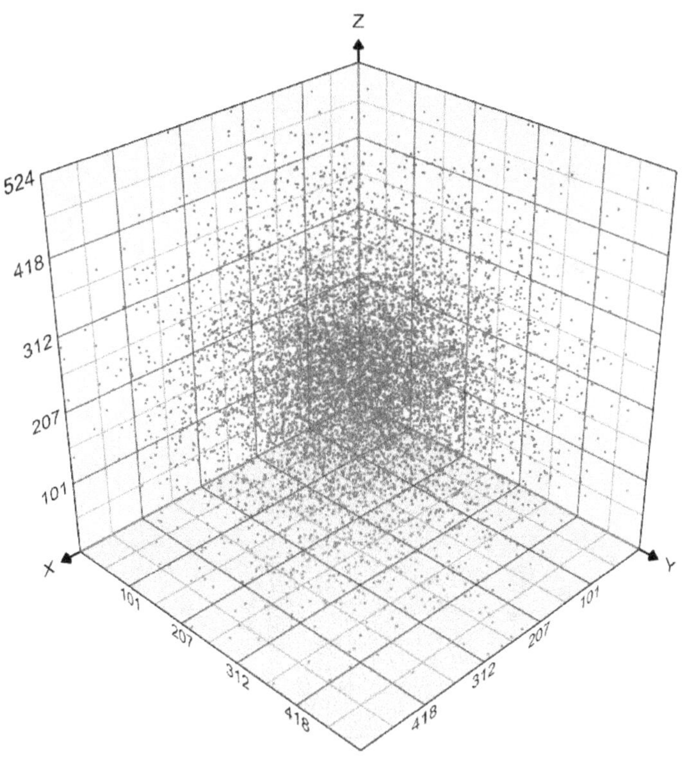

Figure 8-1. Babbling Brook, View #1

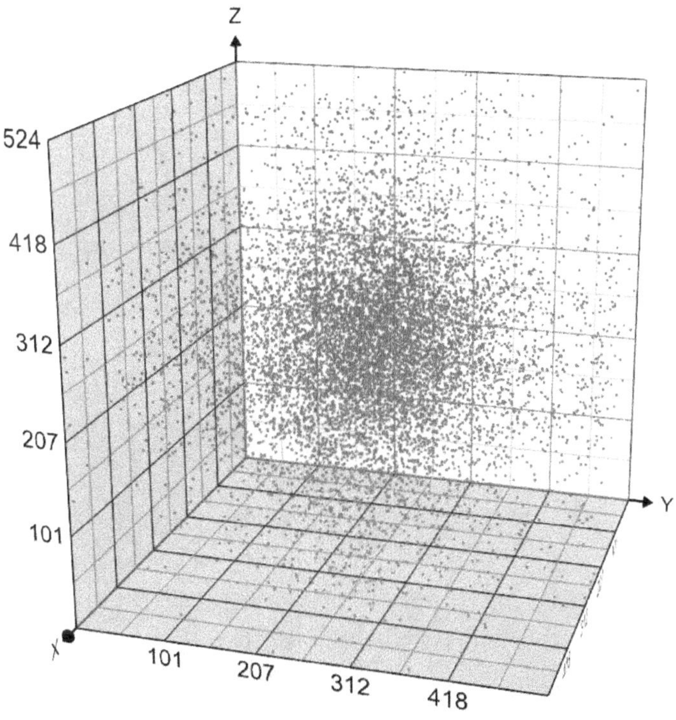

Figure 8-2. Babbling Brook, View #2

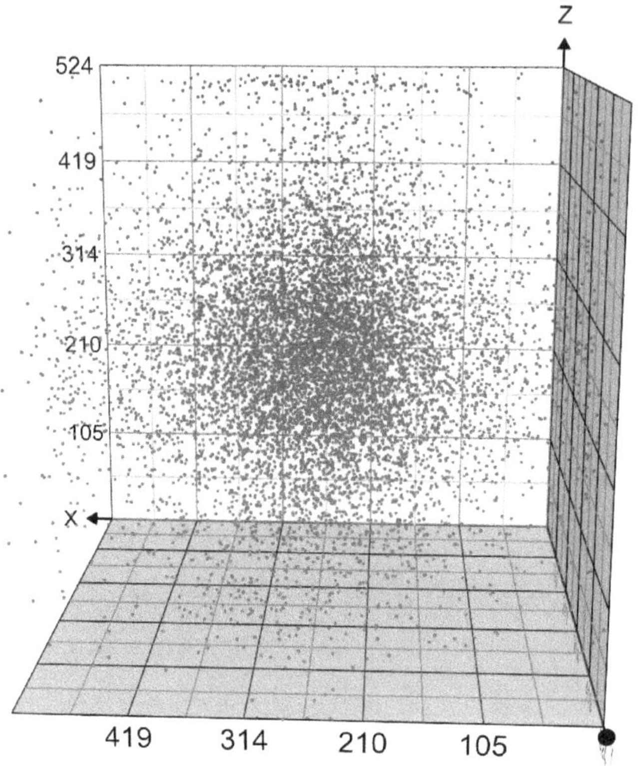

Figure 8-3. Babbling Brook, View #3

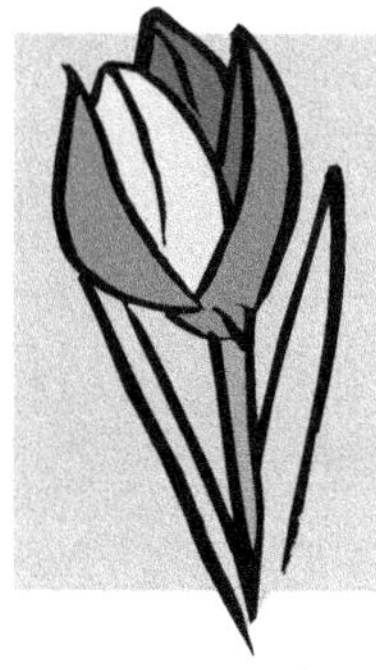

Chapter 9: Dancing Flames

9.1 A Warm Fire on a Cold Winter Night

A fire is always mesmerizing. It might be a campfire when you are out backpacking or a relaxing fire in your fireplace at home. There's something about the dancing flames that captivates us. I especially love a fire in my wood-burning stove on a cold and damp evening. It might be nasty outside, but it's nice and cozy in my living room!

This is an ancient fascination. Archeologists have found evidence of fire in ancient cave dwellings. So what is it that that fascinates us so much? Certainly, like our cave dwelling ancestors, we appreciate the warmth of a fire.

But what is the mesmerizing effect? Are there any patterns in the flames or are they relaxing because of their randomness. There are some factors at play. Here are a few that come to mind:

1. The size of the material that is burning.
2. Its density, as in paper, kindling, hard wood, etc.
3. Its chemical or mineral composition.
4. How far you have the flu open.

Let's capture the light from a fire and see if any patterns emerge.

9.2 The Sensor

For this experiment we will use the same "telescope" (really just a telescope tube without any lenses) and eyepiece arrangement that we used for the "Light on the Water" project of Chapter 7. I had the telescope pointed at the top of the flames where there were a lot of fluctuations.

9.3 Displaying the Data Set

When viewing these plots keep in mind that we are just capturing light levels. Of course it is a very complex event, but the flames repeatedly return to certain light levels.

Figures 9-1 through 9-3 resemble the plots from the "Light on the Water" experiment because there are similar attractors involved. Think about the similarity between blowing wind, flowing water, and convection currents. Water flows downhill because of gravitational attraction, and hot gases are buoyed up due to their decreased density. The same principle applies while enjoying a ride in a hot air balloon.

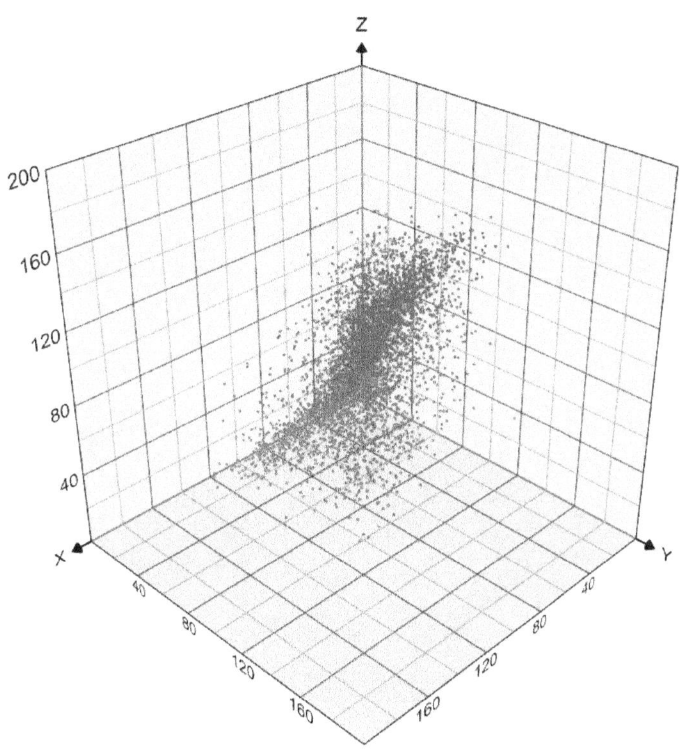

Figure 9-1. Dancing Flames, View #1

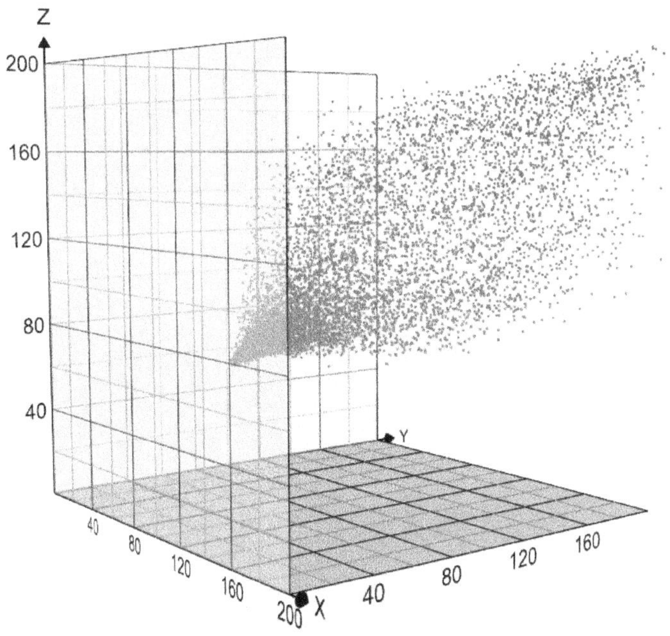

Figure 9-2. Dancing Flames, View #2

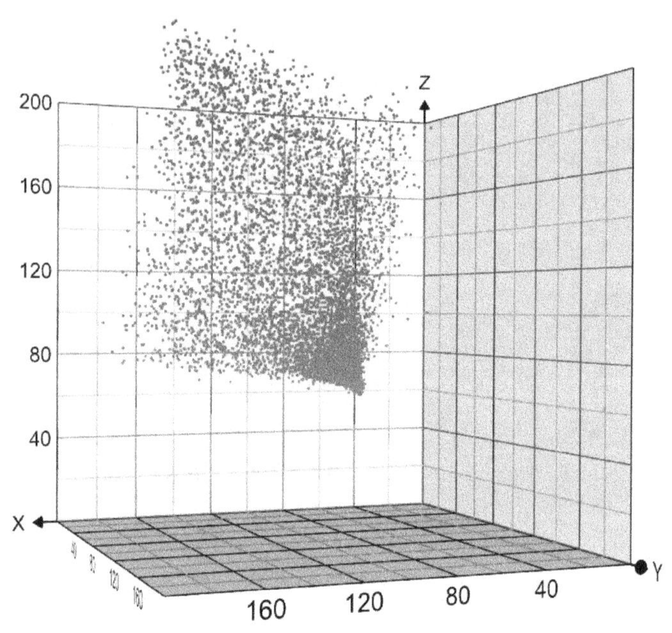

Figure 9-3. Dancing Flames, View #3

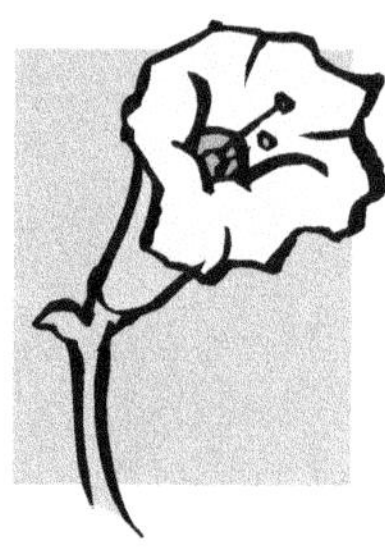

Chapter 10: Waves and Washboards

10.1 They're Everywhere!

Similar wave-like patterns can be found in very different natural events. The medium and the forces involved may be completely different, but there are underlying forces that produce similar formations in these diverse phenomena.

It's amazing! Can waves in a lake be somehow related to washboards on a dirt road, or twigs washing down the side of a hill? Are the underlying attractors the same for freezing dirt and clouds in the sky?

Another thing that amazes me is the apparent regularity in these events. If some twigs are being washed down the side of a hill, I can understand that a twig may get hung up on something and then other twigs will start to pile up behind it, but where does the regularity come from?

Figures 10-1 through 10-4 show some natural phenomena that are very different and yet very much the same.

Figure 10-1. Clouds over Prescott, Arizona

Figure 10-2. Washboard on Thumb Butte Road

Figure 10-3. Frozen Dirt

Figure 10-4. Twigs Washing down a Hillside

10.2 Capturing Wave Motion

All of these events exhibit fairly regular patterns, so we should expect some interesting structure to show up in the plots. The most direct way to measure wave motion is to float a GY-521 accelerometer on the surface of a lake.

I wanted to stick the accelerometer right into the water and let it be buffeted around. Of course, I needed to keep it dry. As shown in Figures 10-5 and 10-6, I cut a hole in a plastic bottle top and then sealed it up with hot glue.

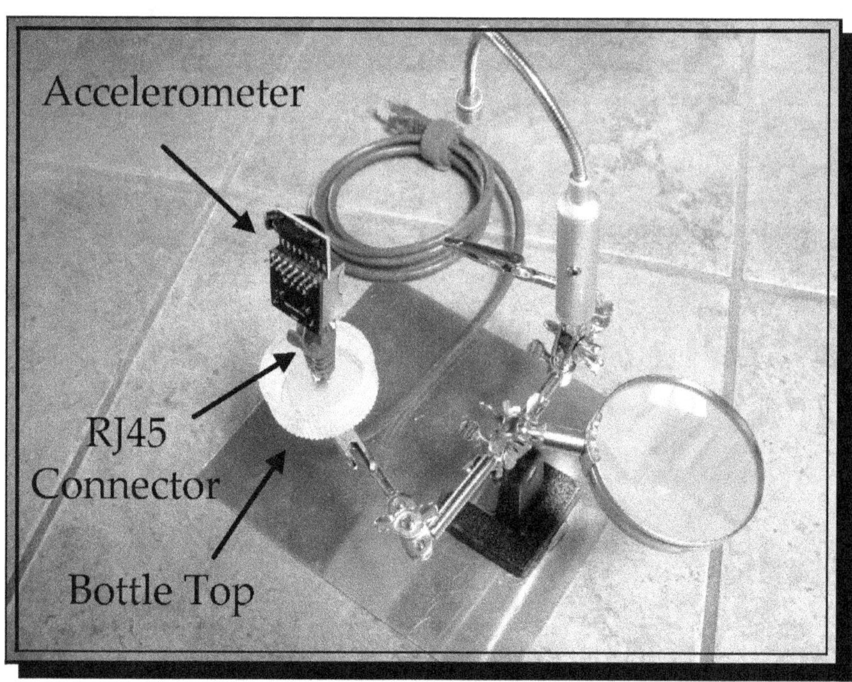

Figure 10-5. Sealing Bottle Top with Hot Glue

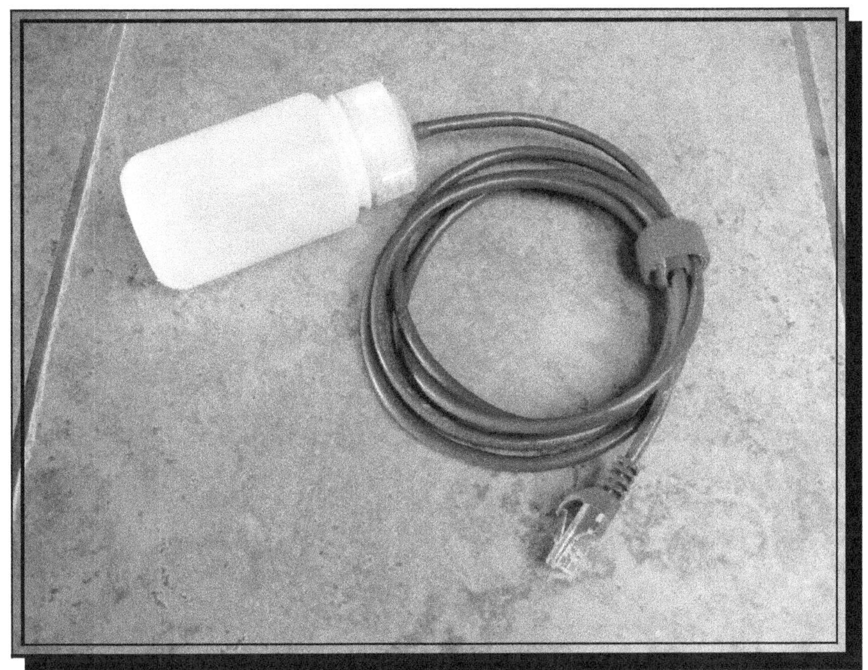

Figure 10-6. Accelerometer Sealed in Plastic Bottle

To measure wave motion I took two different approaches:

1. Float the sensor where it is free to move.
2. Lay the sensor on the shore right where the waves are breaking.

This may seem pretty crude, but to float the accelerometer I simply threw it over a log near the shore as shown in Figure 10-7.

Figure 10-7. Accelerometer Floating on Surface

About half way through the capture some big waves came along and washed it off the log as shown in Figure 10-8. So I thought, "No big deal, let's just let it go and see how it affects the plot." Before looking, can you guess what affect it had? Figures 10-10 through 10-12 display the results.

Figure 10-8. Accelerometer Moved During Capture

For the second dataset I wanted to capture the waves right where they were breaking on the shore. So I put a little stick in the water to keep the accelerometer from washing up on shore as shown in Figure 10-9.

Figure 10-9. Measuring Breaking Waves

10.3 Displaying the Data Sets

Because there is an obvious regularity to the wave motion, I was not surprised by the plots. Figures 10-10 through 10-12 reflect the gentle up and down motion the accelerometer was experiencing, and Figures 10-13 through 10-15 show how it was being washed back and forth in the breaking waves.

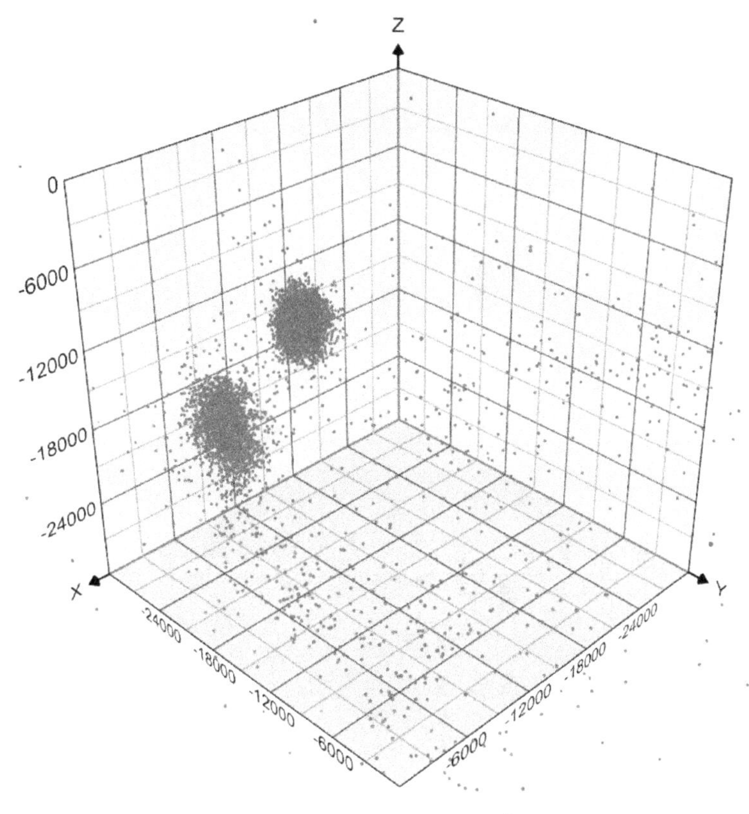

Figure 10-10. Floating Accelerometer, View #1

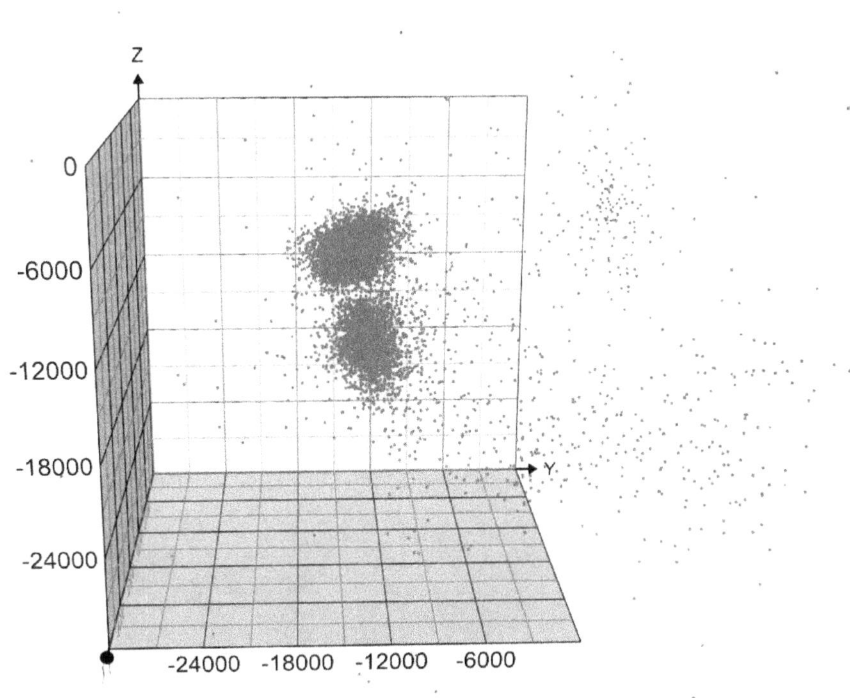

Figure 10-11. Floating Accelerometer, View #2

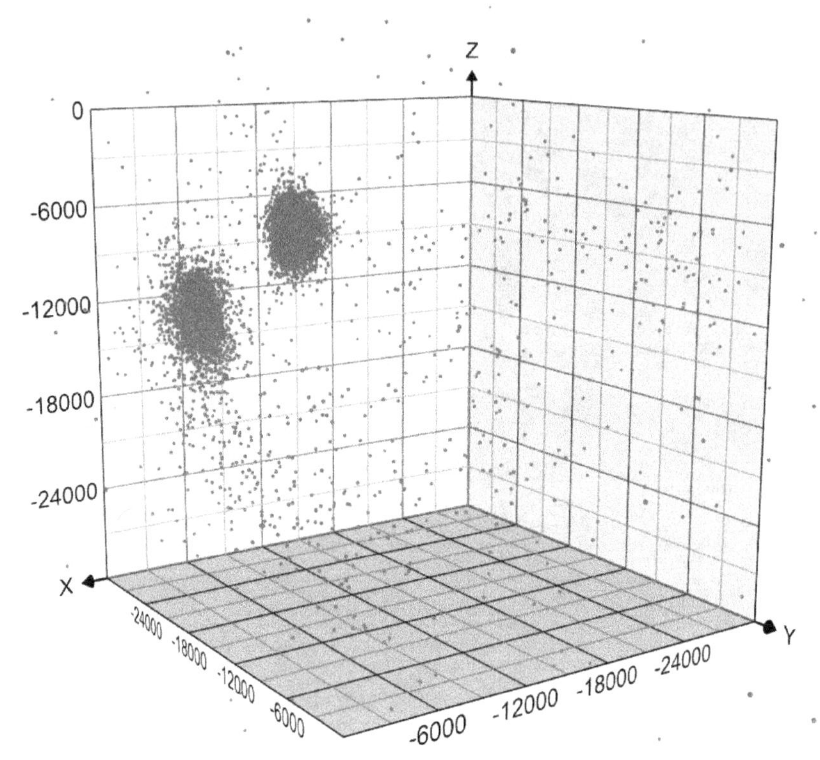

Figure 10-12. Floating Accelerometer, View #3

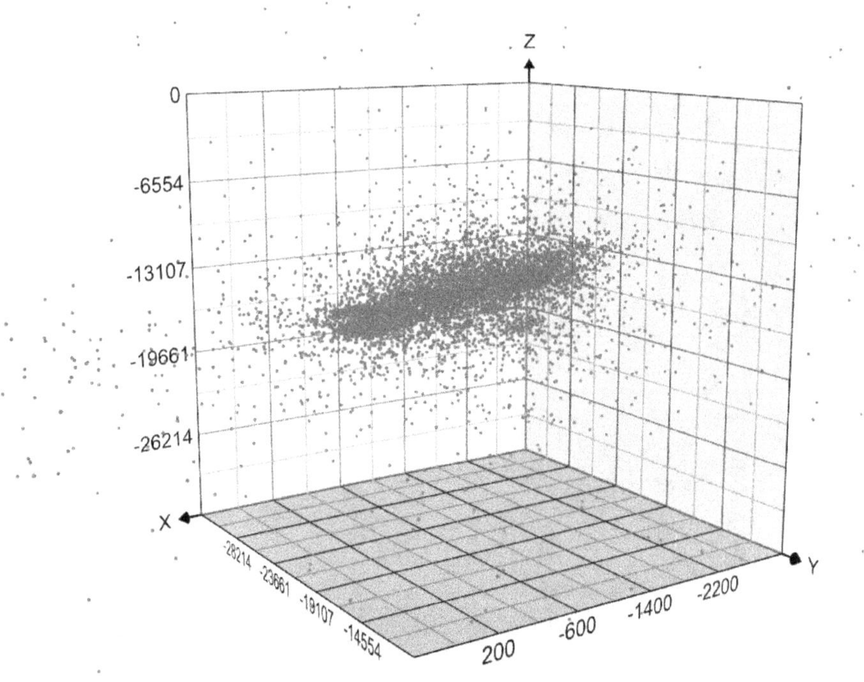

Figure 10-13. Breaking Waves, View #1

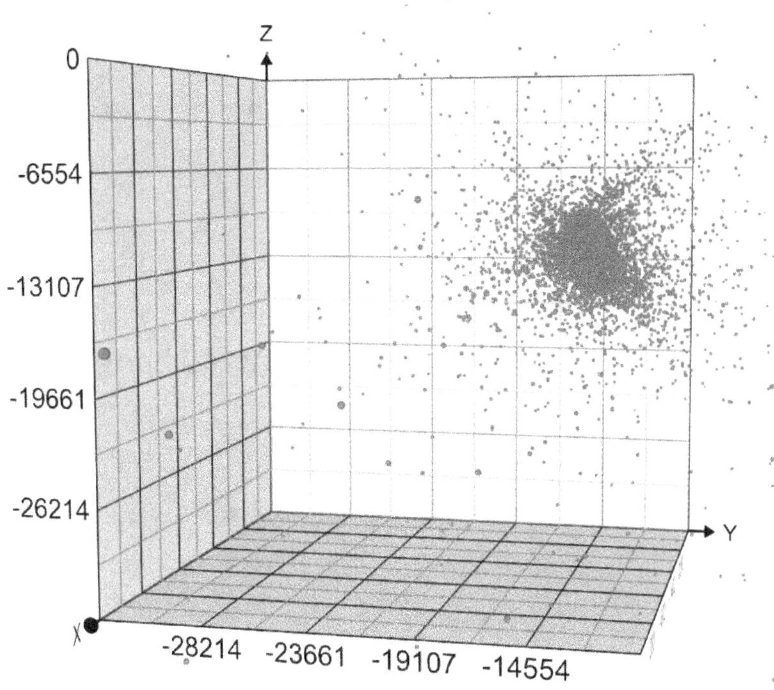

Figure 10-14. Breaking Waves, View #2

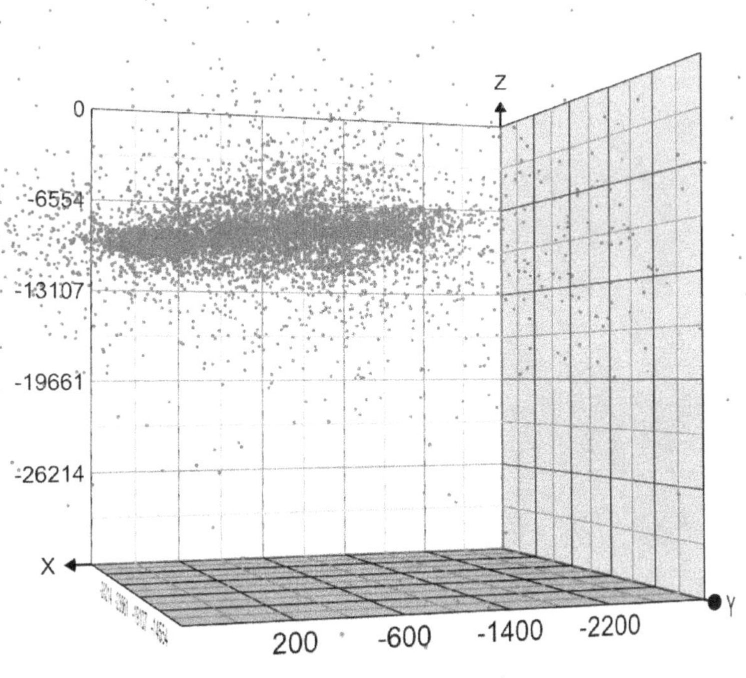

Figure 10-15. Breaking Waves, View #3

What beautiful patterns! Can you see why they look as they do?

Remember how some big waves washed the accelerometer off the log during the first capture cycle?

Looking at Figures 10-10 through 10-12, can you see what happen? Keep in mind these graphs represent 10,000 readings taken over a three and a half minute period. So, we are kind of compressing all those readings into one 3-D picture.

It's amazing to me how capturing some aspects of nature can give us deeper insights!

Chapter 11: Raindrops

11.1 Raindrops Have to Be Random, Right?

If raindrops aren't random, what is? OK, I'm not going to be fooled, or jump to superficial conclusions. So many natural phenomena are very complex but still exhibit the influence of attractors. All of nature is interconnected by a web of powerful forces. Nature is just that way.

One lesson you will learn from this book is that everything in nature is interconnected.
That includes us. We are part of nature and need to learn how to live in harmony with this beautiful blue planet!

11.2 The Sensor

This might seem a little strange, but the vent pipe on my kitchen stove has a cap on the top that magnifies the sound of raindrops. As a storm cell rolls in I hear a few drops, and then a few more, and then the pace picks up until they become indistinguishable. To record the drops from an approaching storm all I have to do is set up my Zoom H2 recorder on the stovetop. If the recording isn't loud enough I can always boost the speaker volume while playing it back on the computer. So, capturing the sound of raindrops is actually pretty simple.

11.3 Displaying the Data Set

In order to capture the time intervals between drops I used the same Schmitt trigger and Arduino sketch as in Section 3.3 of the Dripping Faucet project.

Looking at the plots of Figures 11-1 through 11-3, I am pretty sure the drops are randomly spaced. Of course they are clustered at the lower millisecond values because, as the storm intensified, they were falling quickly. I believe all the widely spaced (high value) outliers represent the drops as the storm cell was just approaching. Even these drops appear to be randomly spaced. As in the white noise and waterfall plots, I don't see any structure.

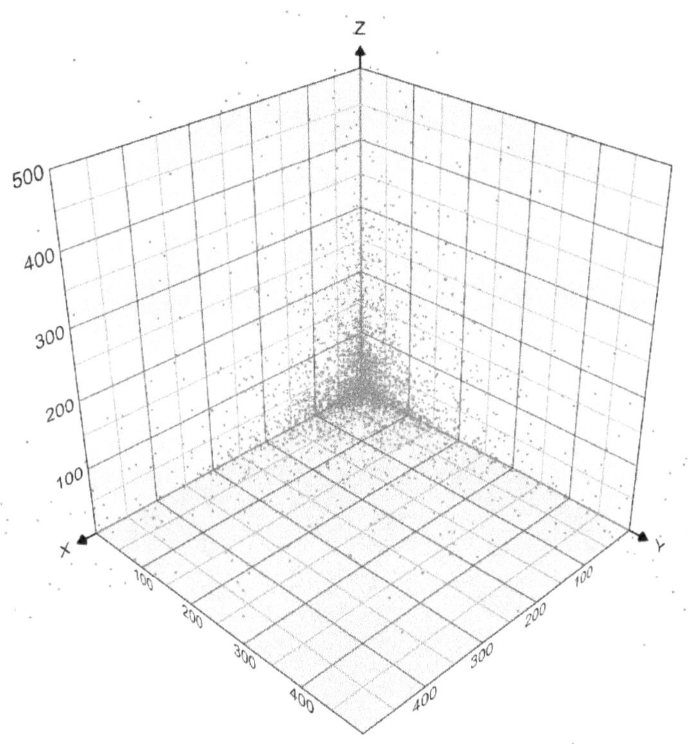

Figure 11-1. Raindrops, View #1

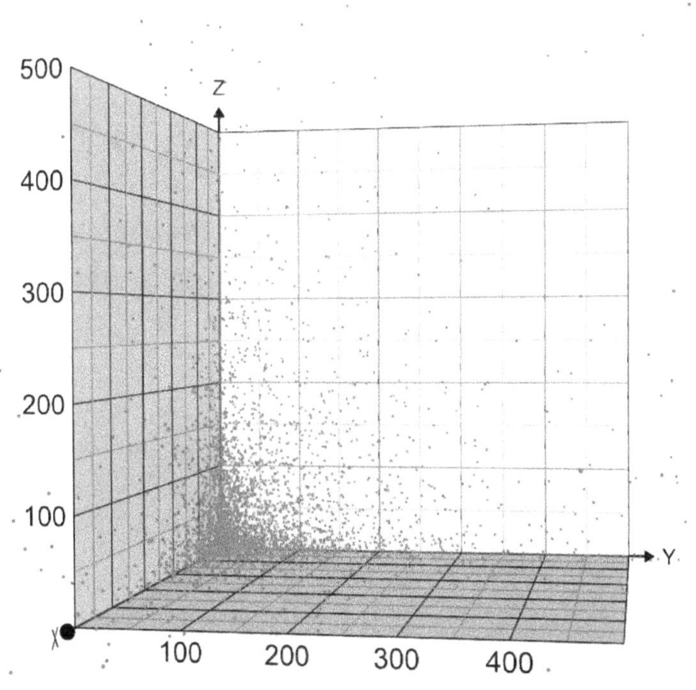

Figure 11-2. Raindrops, View #2

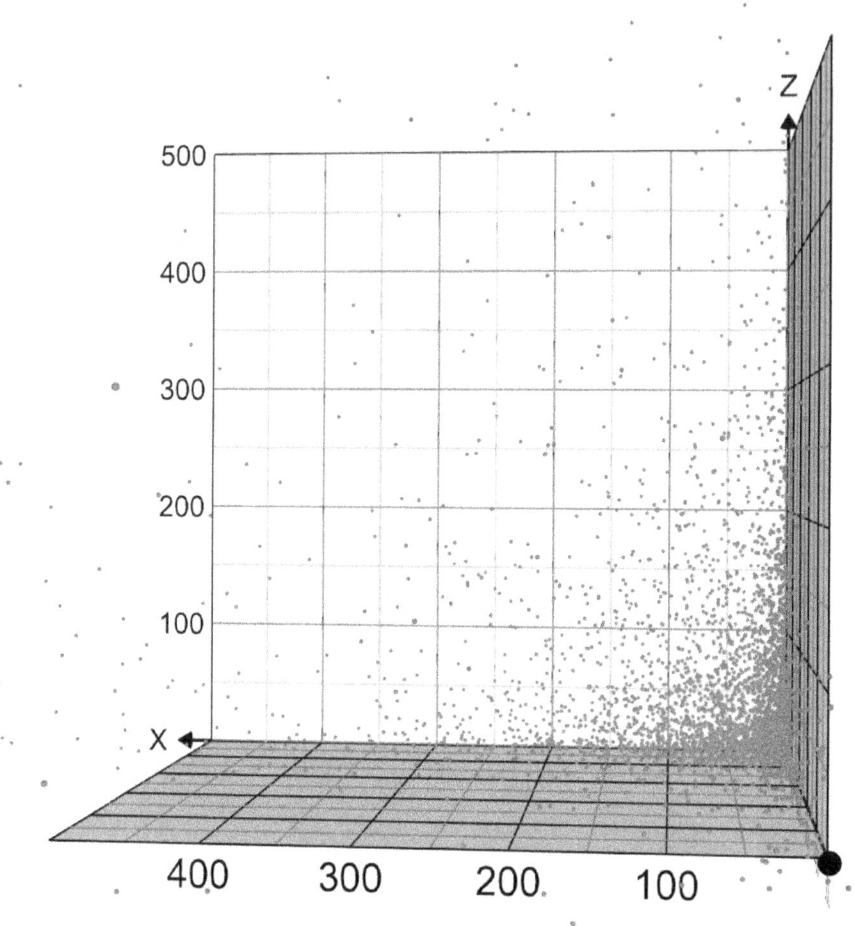

Figure 11-3. Raindrops, View #3

Chapter 12: The Adventure Continues

12.1 Where Do We Go from Here?

In this book we have looked at several different natural phenomena with an eye to discovering patterns. Many of them seemed random or very complex but actually had some underlying pattern because of the forces acting on them. Some of the other events were actually random! Hopefully this brief introduction will whet your appetite so you will continue the adventure and investigate many more aspects of nature. You may want to use different sensors, build different jigs, or use different methods to display and analyze your data.

I would love to hear about your discoveries. Send me an email at rmckeon5@gmail.com.

12.2 Postscript: We Are the Stewards

We are the stewards of this beautiful blue planet. The more we understand and appreciate the complex interrelationships and amazing beauty of the natural world, the more we are inspired to leave it as a place of wonder and discovery for our grandchildren and their grandchildren!

I hope these experiments have been interesting, and in some way have contributed a little bit to that "joie de vivre" that makes life worth living and our beautiful home worth preserving. Be passionate about appreciating and preserving Nature's Hidden Patterns.

Appendix A: Arduino Sketch for Analog Capture

```
/*
This example shows how to log data from an analog sensor
to an SD card. We will be logging from A0 and capturing 10,000 samples.

The circuit:
 SD card attached to SPI bus as follows:
* MOSI - pin 11
* MISO - pin 12
* CLK - pin 13
* CS - pin 4 (for SD Shield 3.0)

created  24 Nov 2010
modified 9 Apr 2012 by Tom Igoe
modified 25 Feb 2018 by Rick McKeon
Public domain
*/

#include <SPI.h>
#include <SD.h>
const int chipSelect = 4;
unsigned long i;

void setup() {
  // Open serial communications
  Serial.begin(9600);
  // wait for serial port to open
  while (!Serial) {}

  Serial.println("Initializing SD card...");
```

```arduino
  // see if the card is present and can be initialized
  if (!SD.begin(chipSelect)) {
    Serial.println("Card failed, or not present");}
    Serial.println("SD card initialized.");


// If "datalog.txt" already exists, delete it.
// This will guarantee we start with a clean datalog.txt file
if (SD.exists("datalog.txt")){
Serial.println("datalog.txt exists");}
if (SD.remove("datalog.txt") == true){
Serial.println("Successfully removed.");}
else
{Serial.println("Could not remove file.");}

  //We are going to capture 10K samples and then stop.
    i = 0;
    while (i < 10000)
    {
      i = i + 1;
// The sensor value is going to be an analogRead from A0
int sensor = analogRead(0);
// Create a file on the SD card that we can write to.
    File dataFile = SD.open("datalog.txt", FILE_WRITE);
    // If the dataFile has been successfully created
    // go ahead and write to it.
  if (dataFile) {
    dataFile.println(sensor);
    // Close the dataFile.
    dataFile.close();
    // Print to the serial port too
    Serial.println(sensor);

  }    else {
    Serial.println("error opening datalog.txt");
```

```
    }
  }
  Serial.println ("sampling finished.");
  }

void loop() {}
```

Appendix B: Arduino Sketch for Interrupt Based Capture

```
/*
After we setup a few things the main loop is empty. It just sets there
waiting for the next interrupt. So, after the setup, all the action is in the
interrupt called "saveTime."

sketch name = "timing_interrupts.ino"
This sketch will time the interval (in milliseconds) since the last rising edge
for interrupt 0 (pin 2) and save that time interval to an SD card. We will
also send it to the serial port so we can see what's happening.

Note: interrupt 0 is on pin 2, but it's the third pin from the end because we
start counting digital pins with zero (pretty strange, but that's how it
works).

SD card attached to SPI bus as follows:
* MOSI - pin 11
* MISO - pin 12
* CLK - pin 13
* CS - pin 4 (for SD Shield 3.0)

Public Domain
*/

#include <SPI.h>
#include <SD.h>
const int chipSelect = 4;
const int interruptPin = 2;
unsigned long previousMillis;

void setup() {
  pinMode(interruptPin, INPUT);
```

```cpp
  attachInterrupt(0, saveTime, RISING);

  // Open serial communications
  Serial.begin(9600);
  // wait for serial port to open
  while (!Serial) {}
  Serial.println("Initializing SD card...");
  // see if the card is present and can be initialized
  if (!SD.begin(chipSelect)) {
    Serial.println("Card failed, or not present");
    }
    Serial.println("SD card initialized.");

  // If "datalog.txt" already exists, go ahead and delete it. This will guarantee
  // that we start with a clean datalog.txt file.
  // If we don't delete it the new data will be appended to the existing file.
  if (SD.exists("datalog.txt")){
  Serial.println("datalog.txt exists");
  if (SD.remove("datalog.txt") == true){
    Serial.println("datalog.txt successfully removed.");
    Serial.println("Start sampling.");}
  else {
  Serial.println("Could not remove file.");
  return;} // stop at this point
  }
  }


void loop () {} // the main loop is empty just waiting for the next interrupt

void saveTime() {
// The "saveTime" interrupt determines time passed since the last interrupt,
// records it to the SD card, and sends it to the serial monitor

// Declare timePassed
```

```
unsigned long timePassed;
// Determine the interval (in milliseconds) since the last interrupt
timePassed = millis() - previousMillis;
//Print the interval to the serial port
Serial.println (timePassed);

// create a file on the SD card that we can write to
  File dataFile = SD.open("datalog.txt", FILE_WRITE);
  // if the dataFile has been successfully created, go ahead and write to it
 if (dataFile) {
  dataFile.println(timePassed);
  // close the dataFile
  dataFile.close();
  previousMillis = millis(); // update previousMillis
}
}
```

Appendix C: Arduino Sketch for Capturing GY-521 Data

```
// MPU-6050 Short Example Sketch
// By Arduino User John Chi, August 17, 2014
// Modified by Rick McKeon, April 1, 2018
// Capture raw accelerometer data and store it
// on an SD card as a 3-column csv file
// Public Domain

#include<SPI.h>
#include<SD.h>
#include<Wire.h>
const int chipSelect = 4; // chip select for the SD card
unsigned long i;
// i is the number of samples (10,000) or trips around the "while" loop
const int MPU_addr=0x68;  // I2C address of the MPU-6050
int16_t AcX,AcY,AcZ,Tmp,GyX,GyY,GyZ; // we only use AcX, AcY, AcZ

void setup(){
  Wire.begin();
  Wire.beginTransmission(MPU_addr);
  Wire.write(0x6B);  // PWR_MGMT_1 register
  Wire.write(0);     // set to zero (wakes up the MPU-6050)
  Wire.endTransmission(true);

  Serial.begin(9600); // open serial communications
  while (!Serial) {} // wait for serial port to open
  Serial.println("Initializing SD card . . .");
  // see if the card is present and can be initialized
  if (!SD.begin(chipSelect)){
```

```cpp
Serial.println("Card failed or is not present.");}
Serial.println("SD card initialized.");

// if "datalog.csv" already exists, delete it
// this will guarantee we start with a clean datalog.csv file
  if (SD.exists("datalog.csv")){
  Serial.println("datalog.csv exists");}
  if (SD.remove("datalog.csv") == true){
  Serial.println("Successfuly removed.");}
  else {Serial.println("Could not remove file.");}

// we are going to capture 10,000 samples and then stop
// all the capture takes place in the setup (executed just once)
// and the main loop is empty

  i = 0;
  while (i < 10000){
  Wire.beginTransmission(MPU_addr);
  Wire.write(0x3B);  // starting with register 0x3B (ACCEL_XOUT_H)
  Wire.endTransmission(false);
  Wire.requestFrom(MPU_addr,6,true);  // request a total of 6 registers
  AcX=Wire.read()<<8|Wire.read();
  // 0x3B (ACCEL_XOUT_H) & 0x3C (ACCEL_XOUT_L)
  AcY=Wire.read()<<8|Wire.read();
  // 0x3D (ACCEL_YOUT_H) & 0x3E (ACCEL_YOUT_L)
  AcZ=Wire.read()<<8|Wire.read();
  // 0x3F (ACCEL_ZOUT_H) & 0x40 (ACCEL_ZOUT_L)

  // create a csv data string for storing to the SD card
  String dataString = String(AcX) + "," + String(AcY) + "," + String(AcZ);
  // create a csv file on the SD card we can write to
  File dataFile = SD.open("datalog.csv", FILE_WRITE);

// if the dataFile has been successfully created go ahead and write to it.
```

```
  if (dataFile) {
    dataFile.println(dataString);
      dataFile.close(); // close the dataFile
      Serial.println(dataString); // print the string to serial port too
      i = i + 1;} // increment i
    else{
      Serial.println("error opening datalog.csv");}}
Serial.println("sampling finished.");
  }


// the setup is executer just once and the main loop is empty
  void loop(){}
```

Appendix D: BASIC Routine for File Conversion

```
REM This routine reads consecutive numbers from a single column matrix
REM called "1-column.txt" on the F drive and writes them to a three
REM column csv matrix called "3-columns.csv"
REM I am using a thumb drive as the F drive just because it is convenient.
REM You may choose to manage files differently.

OPEN "F:\1-column.txt" FOR INPUT AS #1
comma$ = ","
INPUT #1, x 'get first x value
INPUT #1, y 'get first y value
FOR i = 1 TO 9990 'something less than the 10K samples
   INPUT #1, z 'get next z value
   OPEN "F:\3-columns.csv" FOR APPEND AS #2
REM write the 3 values (together with the commas) to file "3-column.csv"
   PRINT #2, x; comma$; y; comma$; z
CLOSE #2
   x = y
   y = z
NEXT i
PRINT "conversion finished"
```

Appendix E: BASIC Routine for Generating Random Numbers

```
REM This routine saves a 1x10,010 random number matrix called
REM  "1-column.txt" on the F drive

DIM n AS INTEGER
RANDOMIZE TIMER ' reseed the random number generator
OPEN "F:\1-column.txt" FOR APPEND AS #1
FOR i = 1 TO 10010
    n = INT(RND * 1023) + 1 'generate a random number between 0 and 1023
    PRINT #1, n 'write the next random number to the file "1-column.txt"
NEXT i
CLOSE #1
PRINT "random number matrix complete"
```

Appendix F: Graphing Calculator 3D

The Graphing Calculator 3D program is easy to use, intuitive, and creates beautiful 3-D scatter plots. It can also create amazing surface plots with highlights and shadows, and a variety of other interesting graphs. It's not free, but I found it worth the cost to create the graphics for this book.

Figure F-1 is the Graphing Calculator 3D home page at
https://runiter.com/graphing-calculator/

Figure F-2 shows the workspace that you see when you first open the program. It is very intuitive, easy to navigate, and responsive. Figures F-3 through F-6 show a sphere ($x^2 + y^2 + z^2 = r^2$) rendered in different ways.

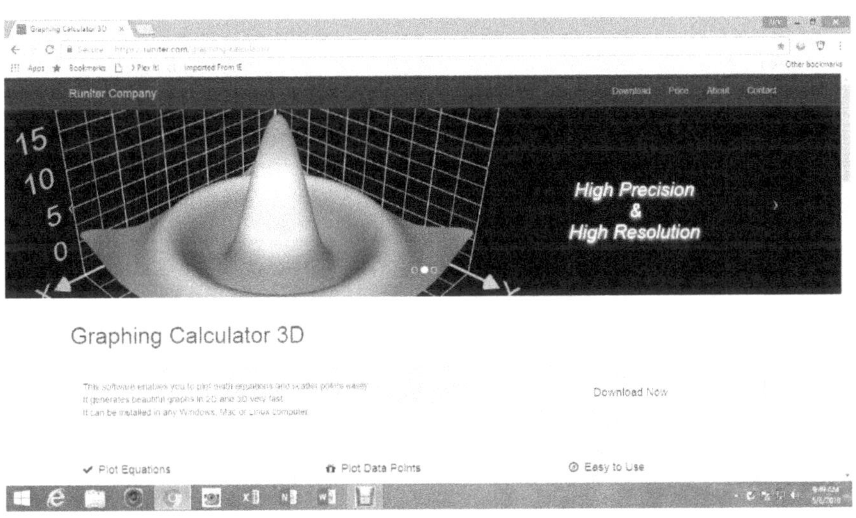

Figure F-1. Graphing Calculator 3D Homepage

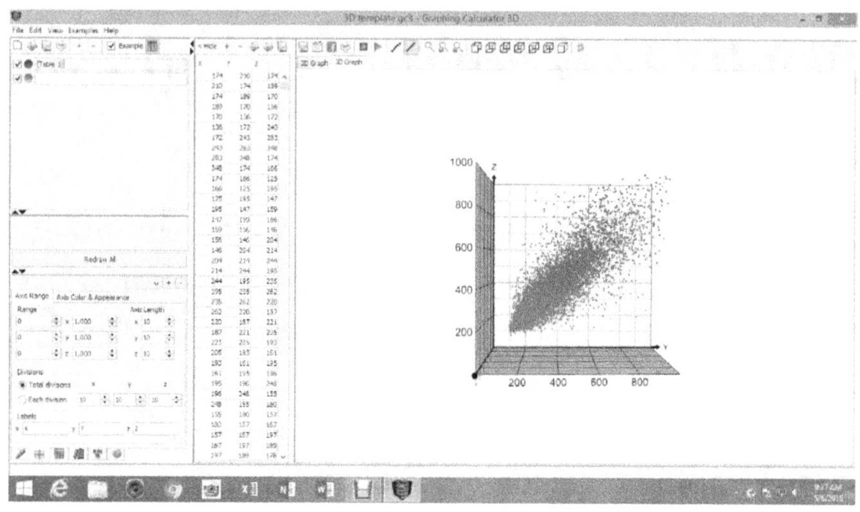

Figure F-2. Graphing Calculator 3D Workspace

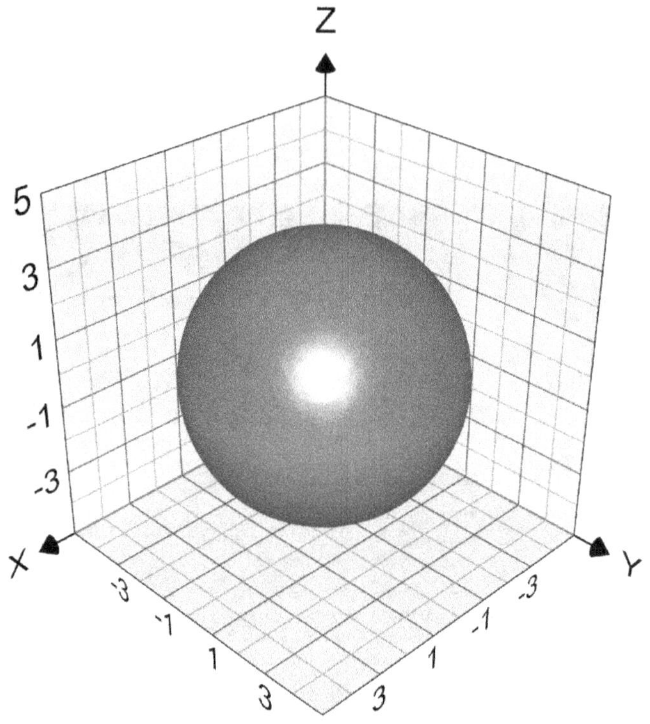

Figure F-3. Sphere Rendered as Surface Plot

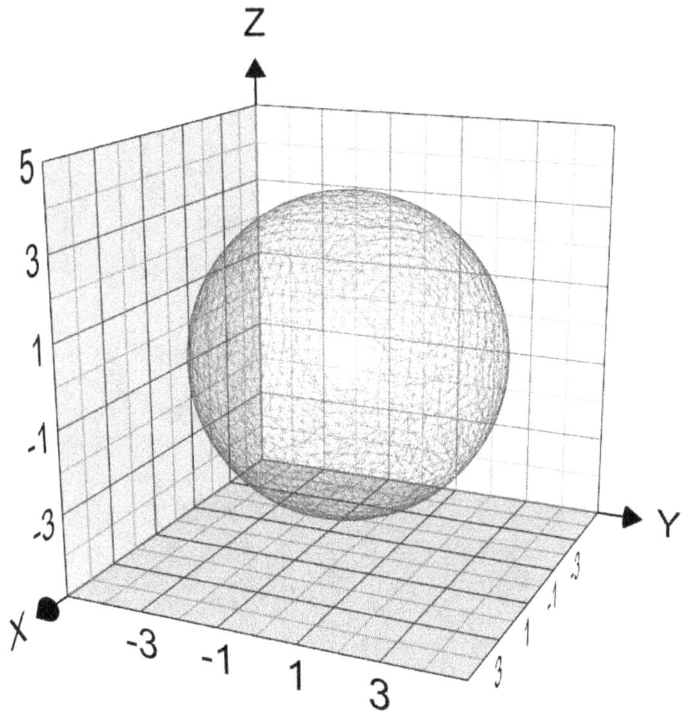

Figure F-4. Sphere Rendered as Lines

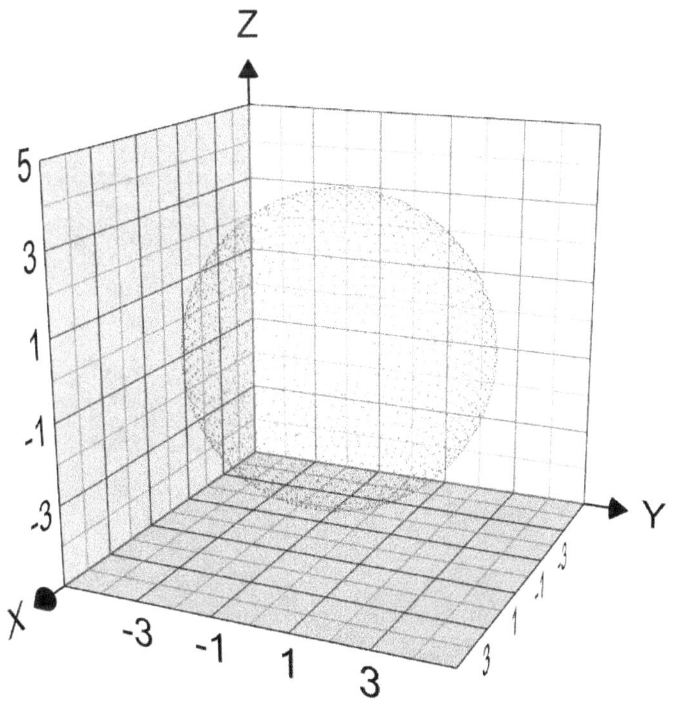

Figure F-5. Sphere Rendered as Points

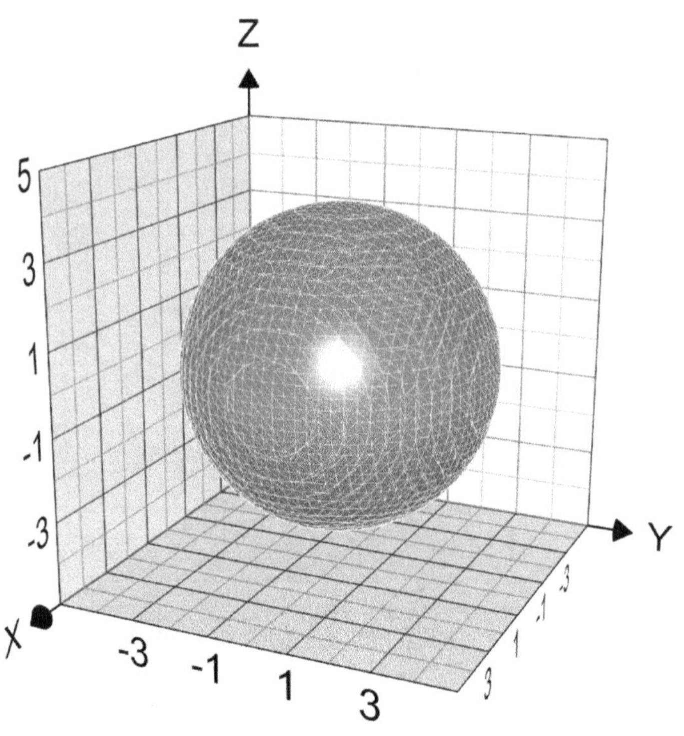

Figure F-6. Sphere Rendered as Wireframe

Meet The Author

Rick holds degrees in both Mathematics and Electrical Engineering. He worked as an engineer designing microprocessor based products, teaching clients, and installing communication networks.

He now lives in beautiful Prescott, Arizona. Since retiring he has been spending time pursuing his passion for writing, playing music and teaching. Rick is currently producing a series of books on music, nature and science.

Some of his other interests include hiking, treasure hunting, recreational mathematics, photography and experimenting with microcontrollers.

For more information about Rick visit his website at rickmckeon.com

Other Books by Rick McKeon

Neural Networks for Electronics Hobbyists: A Non-Technical Project-Based Introduction
ISBN: 978-1-4842-3506-5

Understanding Nature Vol. 1: Enjoying Nature at a Deeper Level!
ISBN: 9341302310020

Understanding Nature Vol. 2: Fun Outdoor Activities for Kids
ISBN: 9341313333234

The Natural Banjo Player: Nature's Lessons for Effortless Playing
ISBN: 9341332924314

The Natural Guitar Player: Nature's Lessons for Effortless Playing
ISBN: 9341333131924

Sierra Impressions: Images and Inspiration From the Sierra Nevada
ISBN: 9341310403499

Underlying Patterns: The Search for Patterns in Nature
ISBN: 9341311343413

You Make Us Feel Young Again! A Collection of Funny and Inspiring Stories from Rest Home Singalongs
ISBN: 9341310334104

Amazing Fractal Images: Postcards From the Complex Plane
ISBN: 9341311990440

Kailee's Adventures in the Pine Forest
ISBN: 9341314293434

Nature's Small World: When Viewed Close up Ordinary Things Become Extraordinary!
ISBN: 9341311943303

www.ingramcontent.com/pod-product-compliance
Lightning Source LLC
Chambersburg PA
CBHW080023260726
48658CB00007B/2445